TOWN & VILLAGE DISCOVERY TRAILS

Yorkshire Dales

Elizabeth Fowler

Published by Sigma Leisure – an imprint of
Sigma Press, 1 South Oak Lane, Wilmslow, Cheshire SK9 6AR, England.

British Library Cataloguing in Publication Data
A CIP record for this book is available from the British Library.

ISBN: 1 85058 491 5

Typesetting and Design by: Sigma Press, Wilmslow, Cheshire.

Cover Design: MFP Design & Print

Cover Photograph: Bainbridge Village Green *(the author)*

Maps and photographs: the author

Printed by: MFP Design & Print

Preface

This is not a lace-up-your-boots-and-go guide. It is essentially a more leisurely look at this most beautiful corner of England. Too often, visitors arrive here and are literally overwhelmed by the sheer physical scale of what confronts them.

I have tried to produce a book that is altogether more laid back than the average walking guide. Firstly, there are no great distances involved. Each can be tackled without hesitation by young families or even by those who bring along the grandparents. Where there are any difficulties to anyone who is not a reasonably active adult, they are noted.

Walking boots are not necessary. A "clean shoe" guide is given indicating the kind of terrain that will be encountered. This starts at 1 for definitely muddy to 10, clean pavements all the way. These are almost all "worst case" ratings. On a clear day with no recent rain, they will all rate 10.

You are encouraged to be inquisitive. Much of what there is to see is hidden from the average tourist who arrives at the car park, spends half an hour looking round and then whizzes off to the next honey trap. To seek out, enquire, and understand is a singularly satisfying experience.

If you are holidaying in the Dales, this book is your perfect companion. The short distances involved, both on foot and between one walk and the next, allow for a pleasurable morning stroll, lunch, a short drive and another Trail in the afternoon.

If you enjoy walking them as much as I enjoyed researching them, you are in for a wonderful time. Good hunting!

Elizabeth Fowler

Location Map

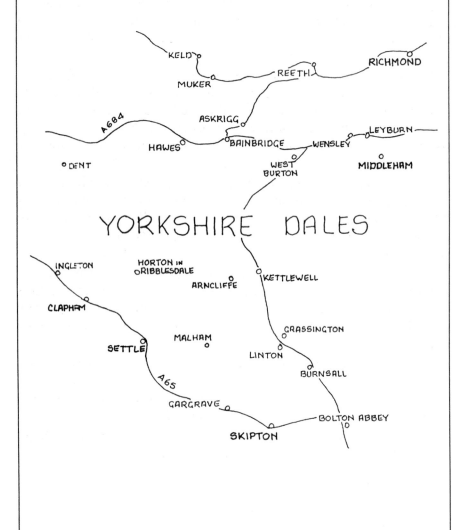

Contents

Introduction

From bosky vales to towering mountain peaks: 680 square miles (1760sq km) of beauty in an infinite variety of forms – that is the Yorkshire Dales National Park. Although it's a place of delicate charm around the lower areas of the rivers Wharfe and Swale, it can also be frighteningly majestic. Three of England's highest mountains can be found within the Park boundary: Whernside (2491ft/736m), Inglebor-ough (2372ft/723m) and Pen-y-ghent (2273ft/695m). Between the extremes, there are delightful villages sustaining ancient customs and attractively diverse buildings.

Remarkably, considering its short history, the first nation to organ-ise the preservation of wild open spaces was the United States. Even more astonishingly, this came about in 1864, at the height of their Civil War, when the Yosemite valley in California was declared a protected area. Eight years later, this was incorporated into Yellow-stone Park. Although it became the basis of ours, their idea was very different. They acquired virgin land as the frontiers pushed west-wards, thus protecting newly-discovered natural beauty from exploi-tation. In England, land was already in private ownership, often as part of great estates which had enough political clout to ensure that their ownership was respected.

Thus, the motive here was twofold: to improve rights of access, and to ensure that any development was strictly controlled. Ownership of the land remained (generally) in private hands, a situation obtain-ing to this day.

The Council for the Preservation of Rural England first proposed the establishment of National Parks in 1929. Given the speed at which our governments move, it was entirely predictable that it took twenty years for this to come to fruition. In 1949, an Act was passed, and the Yorkshire Dales were designated by the resulting Commission in 1954. Several Acts and bureaucratic upheavals later, the Park is administered today by The Yorkshire Dales National Park.

Most of the Trails in this book are in the area covered by the

Yorkshire Dales National Park. Because the boundaries drawn were, by definition, arbitrary, places like Skipton, Leyburn, Middleham and Richmond were left out. But historically, they have always been very much at the heart of Dales culture, scenery and thinking. For those reasons, it was impossible to leave them out of this text. The former and latter are, respectively, the main south and north entrances to the Park and each have a compulsive interest of their own.

Each Trail listed in this book has been carefully researched to provide an accurate description of what is on the ground, accompanied by a look at any historical interest or connection. Sketch maps accompany the route, as an added safeguard against getting lost.

¤   Walk instructions are set in a contrasting style, like this!

Useful Contacts

The Yorkshire Dales National Park, Colvend, Hebden Road, Grassington, Skipton, North Yorkshire BD23 5LB. Tel: 01756 752748. They operate a series of Visitor Centres at:

Aysgarth Falls – 01969 663424

Clapham – 01524 251419

Grassington* – 01756 752774

Hawes* – 01969 667450

Malham* – 01729 – 830363

Sedbergh – 01539 620125

These are all open April to October only, 10am to 5pm. The ones marked * have a teletext screen available 24 hours a day throughout the year.

Maps

The Ordnance Survey "Landranger" sheets at a scale of 1:50,000 (1¼ins to the mile) give full coverage of the Yorkshire Dales. OS also produce a series of Outdoor Leisure maps that cover all the Dales on three sheets: Numbers 2, 10 and 30. These are at twice the scale: 1.25,000 or 2½ inches to a mile. They are excellent value and strongly recommended.

Trail 1: Bolton Abbey

Wharfedale: that most picturesque of valleys carved by the river Wharfe on its 60 mile journey from the moors south of Hawes to Cawood near Tadcaster, where it joins the Ouse.

The first task is to prove that this book is a celebration of the glorious Dales, rather than a formula-driven title. This Trail does just that. The village of Bolton Abbey is rather more a hamlet and the Trail will take much more account of the Abbey and Wharfedale than the (somewhat limited) fabric of Bolton Abbey village.

Trail Facts

Distance: 2½ miles

Clean Shoe Rating: 3

Map: O.S. Landranger Series No 104

Start: Bolton Abbey village Car Park. This is 1 mile north of the A59 Skipton to Harrogate road along the B6160.

Starting Grid Ref: SE 071539

Car Parking: See above

Refreshment: Soon after start, and halfway round

Nearest TIC 9, Sheep Street, Skipton, North Yorkshire BD23 1JH – 01756 792809.

¤ Leave the car park by the main entrance and turn left. On the right is Bolton Abbey Gift Shop, Post Office, Stores and Tea Cottage. A few metres beyond is what can only be described as a hole in the wall. Pass through this and enter the Abbey grounds. The area is honeycombed with tracks, but they are all permissive paths, not Rights of Way.

¤ Follow the clearly marked path down into the valley and bear left towards the bridge. Cross this to the other bank. Or, if you are

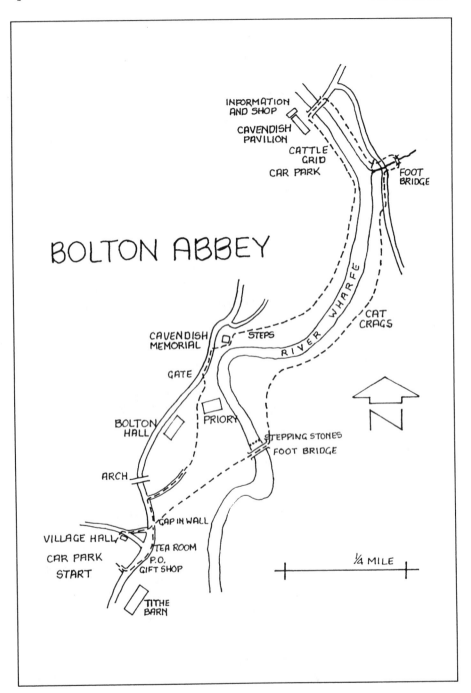

feeling particularly adventurous, gain the far side by using the long line of stepping stones.

¤   Turn left and follow the river bank closely. There are several alternatives which climb out of the valley on the right, but these should be ignored. Shortly the waterside path will climb up above the river along Cat Crags and eventually bear away to a road. Turn left, down to the valley. Ahead is a ford, with a footbridge 30 metres upstream.

¤   Immediately over the stream, turn left back towards the Wharfe and right, over a stone stile just beyond a gate. The path is now of very high quality which continues to the next bridge. Turn left, over the water and at the far end, left again.

This bridge was rebuilt by officers and men of 202 Field Squadron, Royal Engineers V. It was re-opened on January 22nd 1989 by the Marquis of Hartington.

The Cavendish Pavilion offers a good range of food. The Lords Restaurant is open Sunday to Thursday 12 noon to 6pm, 12 noon to 5pm and 6pm to 9pm Fridays and Saturdays. The menu is eclectic and of good quality. The tea room offers a more basic selection, from a pot of tea upwards, also of very acceptable quality. An ice cream stall is also available. More information on 01756 710245.

Next door, a Visitor Centre carries a good range of maps, books and guides, together with the more usual collection of "touristy" souvenirs.

¤   Over a cattle grid, take the left-hand path – the one nearest to the river. This passes through a car park built in delightful water meadows before veering away as a rocky outcrop appears, passing through a gate and up a flight of very unevenly spaced steps to the road. Turn left.

The bloody and turbulent history of Ireland may appear a substantial distance away from this peaceful scene, but one particular act of violence there is commemorated here by the Cavendish Fountain.

In 1882 the prime minister William Gladstone appointed Lord Frederick Cavendish, brother of the 8th Duke of Devonshire as chief secretary for Ireland. Immediately on his arrival, he was in Phoenix

Park, Dublin with his under secretary, Burke, when they were both murdered by a gang of "Irish Invincibles". The fountain that bears his name was erected on this spot in 1886.

¤ Walk down the road for some 300 metres until a gate is reached. This opens into the Abbey grounds. Follow the path down to the remains.

The original religious enclave in this area was established a few miles to the west in Embsay in 1120. The Augustinian friars moved to this, their new site in 1154 following the provision of money by Alice de Romille "...for the well-being of my soul and those of my forbears and descendants.", the development of which was continued right through to the Dissolution.

To accommodate locals for worship, the present nave was added about 1240. The West Tower was left unfinished when the Abbey was closed in 1539. Had it been completed, it would have joined the nave and would have been even more impressive. The modern roof and bell-turret were erected in 1983 to preserve and enhance the tower.

It was a prosperous undertaking, with the friars engaging in sheep rearing. It was clearly a source of plunder because the place was ravaged several times over the years by marauding bands of Scots who made the long journey south. They became such regular visitors that an armed defence force was established to combat the problem.

Because it had also been used by local people for a church, permission to continue worship there was obtained from the Commissioners of Henry VIII. To this day, it is the local priory church of St Mary and St Cuthbert in the diocese of Bradford. There is a service here every Sunday morning at 10.30am.

Brewing beer was a function of priories in those days. Fortunately, records of Bolton Priory's activities in this sphere have been preserved; and startling reading they make.

Given that the whole community of canons, lay-brothers, servants and other dependants only totalled around 200, they brewed 50,000 gallons a year. In addition, they bought in some 600 – 700 gallons of wine each year. And alcohol is a problem today?

¤ Leave the church and turn left. Follow the track around to the right

Memorial to Frederick Cavendish

and back up to the main road. Here, the Trail will turn left, but a few metres around the corner to the right is a fascinating archway spanning the road. 10ft 6ins high and 8ft 6ins across (3.1m x 2.5m), it is something of a hazard to traffic today.

¤ On reaching the Tea Cottage, turn right along the road. A few metres along on the left is the Village Hall with the car park immediately behind.

Across to the right, in private grounds, is Bolton Hall. This was originally the gate-house for the priory, built in the fourteenth century. It was rebuilt to become a house in 1720, being enlarged and substantially rebuilt in 1840 by the famed architect Joseph Paxton.

It's also the place of legend and ghosts. A delightful example of the former concerns its founding and the Boy of Egremond who was a son of Alec de Romille and very fond of hunting. The story goes that whilst out hunting, he drowned in the river. His mother then caused the priory to be founded on that spot in his memory. Sadly, the tale is false; he signed the deeds for the transfer of that very land. But, never let a silly thing like the truth interfere with a good story.

The local rectory, built on the site of the priory kitchen, is haunted by the ghost of a monk. He has been seen many times over the centuries, often by people whose veracity should not be doubted. The Marquis of Hartington made a detailed deposition of his encounter in 1912 and several incumbent priests have been visited.

The priory was the subject of a well-known painting by Sir Edward Landseer (1802-1873). One of our premier artists in the nineteenth century, he is probably best remembered for his magnificent "Monarch of the Glen" painting, and his lion sculptures which still grace Trafalgar Square in London. J.M.W. Turner – he of "The Fighting Téméraire" – was also inspired by the beauty of this area – see Trail 19.

Trail 2: Skipton

The Southern Gateway to the Dales. Thus does Skipton regard itself: and quite rightly too. Here on the east bank of the valley of the river Aire, there is evidence that settlement had taken place by the seventh century. Then known as "Sheeptown", it was soon to become a centre for the woollen trade, a position it held for centuries.

The geographical location of Skipton, first with turnpike roads down into the heart of the West Riding and out to Kendal and early links with Lancashire ensured that it would prosper.

As transport improved, the existence of a cattle market saw a resulting increase in trade. With that, the wool trade increased, all these activities demanding labour. Thus was a large increase in housing noted during this period.

Later, the Leeds and Liverpool Canal would arrive in the town in 1773, providing a link to Bingley, although it would be another

Old warehouses in Skipton, tastefully converted to flats

forty-three years before the through line was open. Canal transport
led to all the new mills being built at the water's edge.

The ascendancy of water transport was soon to fade as the railway
arrived in town during the 1840s. This first provided a link with
Leeds, later being extended towards Hellifield and Ingleton. Eventually, in 1875, Carlisle was reached – see Trail 10. This provided a far
better service and reigned supreme for almost a century before roads
took over.

Today, the town has an effective by-pass taking all the heavy lorries
that once thundered through the town away around the edges. The
street market is active most days in the High Street where an excellent
range of shops will be found.

The railway still operates, a frequent electric service connecting
the town with Bradford and Leeds. Even the canal thrives. There is
one company offering luxurious cruises (with licensed bar). These
are operated by Pennine Boat Trips, The Wharf, Skipton. A call to
01756 790829 will bring details of times and cost.

For the more adventurous, Pennine Cruisers, 19, Coach Street,
Skipton (next door to Pennine Boat Trips) offer self-steer boats for
hire by the day – or longer. They can be contacted on 01756 795478.

Trail Facts

Distance:	1¼ miles
Clean Shoe Rating:	10
Map:	O.S. Landranger Series No 103
Start:	Keighley Road Car Park
Starting Grid Ref:	SD 989515
Car Parking:	As above
Refreshment:	Plenty, all around the town
Nearest TIC	9 Sheep Street, Skipton, N. Yorkshire, BD23 1JH – 01756 792809.

¤ From the car park, walk *away* from the road towards the canal. A
   footbridge crosses the water and leads to the towpath on the far
   bank. On reaching the water's edge, turn left.

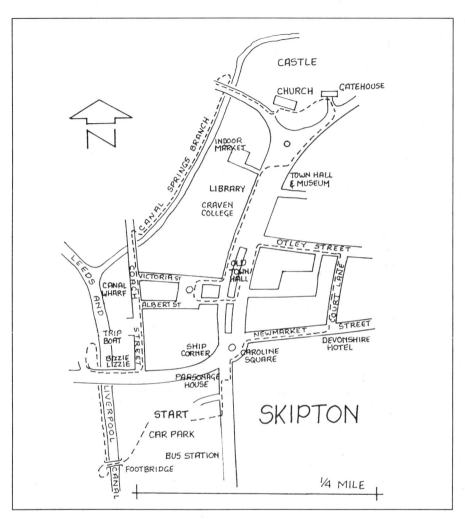

¤　Under the next bridge and the base for boat trips is noted across the water. Leave the canal and walk back to the main road, turning left past "Bizzie Lizzie's", a superb fish and chip emporium.

Harry Ramsden originally defined the quality of this product. Skipton's own has taken it to new heights – and at a reasonable price as well. You can sit in or take them out and stand, watching the canal boats on the bridge whilst you savour this delight.

¤　Immediately over the bridge, turn left into Coach Street. Having eaten your chips, perhaps the delight of a dessert calls. On the left, just past the canal wharf is Skipton Creameries, an ice cream parlour serving a wonderful range of tasty products. Opposite, on the right, is Victoria Street.

Within recent memory, all the housing in this area has been replaced with something more modern. Now, with a few shops and lack of motor vehicles, this, and Victoria Square at the end, are pleasant places to be.

¤ Continue along Coach Street to the canal. Walk a few metres further and on the right is access to the towing path. Turn right, away from the main canal.

This is The Springs Branch, a 770 yard (700m) line that leads into what can only be described as a ravine. It was built by the Earl of Thaney when he was owner of Skipton Castle and limestone quarries nearby.

A horse tramway was built from those quarries to the branch and chutes constructed. These had a drop of some 120ft (36m). Limestone was hurled down these into the waiting canal boats. It must have been a fearfully noisy – to say nothing of dusty – place to work. Now, although the quarries still produce, everything goes by either road or rail.

¤ Walk along the towing path to the first bridge. Pass under this and then turn sharp left to gain the road above. Turn left, and a few metres along is the parish church.

Holy Trinity church is a gaunt, somewhat forbidding building, mainly fourteenth-century and enlarged over the next hundred or so years. There is a wonderful rood screen dated 1534, and tombs of the Clifford family can be found inside.

Next door is Skipton Castle. It was the Normans, spreading north after the Conquest of 1066 that first built a castle here overlooking Eller Beck. Robert de Romille was the knight who started the ball rolling. The Romille name has already been encountered on Trail 1 in connection with Bolton Abbey.

This brooding structure passed into the hands of the Clifford family in 1309. They were responsible for much rebuilding over the centuries. Lady Anne Clifford, last of the family line lived through the Civil War, during which time it was the last Royalist stronghold in the north.

After the conflict, she put in hand repairs that were to leave the castle substantially as it can be seen today, one of the best-preserved and most complete medieval castles in England. It's open to visitors every day except Christmas, admission £3.40 with the usual reductions. Full details on 01756 792442.

¤ **Walk down High Street on the right-hand side. This leads into Sheep Street. Towards the bottom of there, an alleyway on the right leads into Victoria Square.**

This wide area was – and is – the market. Once a weekly event of great importance locally, there are stalls here pretty well every day now.

The office of the local weekly newspaper, The Craven Herald, is one of many attractive buildings along this section. Built well over two hundred years ago, it has seen a number of occupants over the years. It was first used by a cloth trader, William Chippendale (no connection with a group of exotic male dancers – so far as is known). It was taken over by a printer, John Tasker, in 1838 and the first newspaper was produced twenty years later.

This did not last long, as Tasker pursued other business interests, but, by 1874, The Craven Herald was established and this venerable organ has published ever since.

The library was added this century, one of many endowed by the American philanthropist Andrew Carnegie. A much older building is the Black Horse Inn. There is a stone carved with the date 1676 here, but the original building has been much rebuilt and modified to produce what meets the eye today.

It is also necessary to keep an eye on things to the left-hand side of the road. The Town Hall is today the administrative centre of Skipton. In addition, the town museum is located here. Successive buildings along this section all show a grace and elegance once the accepted – and only – way to build. Lots of local stone has created a town of great dignity.

Sheep Street is a cobbled thoroughfare suffering massive overcrowding in the summer. But, if you can find it during a quiet spell, it will reveal much of its glory. Here, and further round this walk, keep your eyes above street level. Some of the most ornate carvings and stone work will be revealed on the first floor and above.

After the activity on the main road, Victoria Square is an oasis of peace – and quite beautiful. Look carefully around as you reach the Square, there is plenty of evidence in the remaining buildings of the antiquity of this area.

¤   Turn around, walk back through the arch and straight across into High Street. Turn left, cross by the pedestrian crossing and take the first right which is Otley Road.

On the left between Sheep Street and High Street is Middle Row. One building, with the ornate flight of steps up to the tourist office is the old town hall. Built in the late eighteenth century, it once housed the local exchequer where rent payments were made. It has also acted variously as a court, prison, mechanics institute and home for council meetings.

¤   Now, take the second right into Court Lane. On the corner is Craven Court Shopping Centre with a beautifully ornate octagonal iron staircase with wood cappings, the whole decorated green.

Across the way, a carefully painted and well cleaned Royal crest sits proudly over Skipton County Court. There is one particularly impressive building on the left. This was once a barn and the now blocked archway was where horse and cart would enter.

¤   At the bottom is Newmarket Street: turn right.

The graceful Georgian Devonshire Hotel is then encountered on the left. Built in 1731 as a town house, it was converted to a hotel in 1790, acquiring its present name in 1810.

¤   At the end is Caroline Square. Here, turn left into Keighley Road and use the pedestrian crossing after a few metres to reach the other side.

Across the road from Caroline Square, at the corner of Swadford Street, the row of shops there are accommodated in Central Buildings. This was once the parsonage house for Christ Church, Skipton.

¤   Turn right at the end of the shops into the car park.

Trail 3: Burnsall

T his is little more than a stroll through an exceedingly pretty village, preceded by another look at the river Wharfe. For all its shortness, it has beauty, interest and history packed tightly. Overlooking the scene, Bardon Moor looks down admiringly.

Trail Facts

Distance: ¾ mile

Clean Shoe Rating: 3

Map: O.S. Landranger Series No 98

Start: Burnsall village car park, alongside the river Wharfe.

Starting Grid Ref: SE 031612

Car Parking: As above

Refreshment: Tea room at the start, pub towards the end, together with another tea room.

Nearest TIC National Parks Centre, Hebden Road, Grassington, N. Yorkshire BD23 5LB – 01756 752748.

¤ From the car park, walk towards the river's edge and turn left – upstream. Ahead, the attractive bridge which takes the road towards Appletreewick – see at the foot of this Trail.

The present bridge was erected in the 1880s, successor to many that had been built over the centuries only to be ravaged by flood water streaming down the valley.

¤ At the foot of this bridge, steps lead down, taking the path under the stonework via the river bed. When there is a degree of "fresh" coming down, the water may wash over this. Then, walk up to the road, cross, and pick the Trail up at the other side. From here, the footpath alongside the water is clearly defined and fenced.

This takes the Trail along the back of Burnsall. When it was built, the houses tended to front the road and the less attractive parts faced the

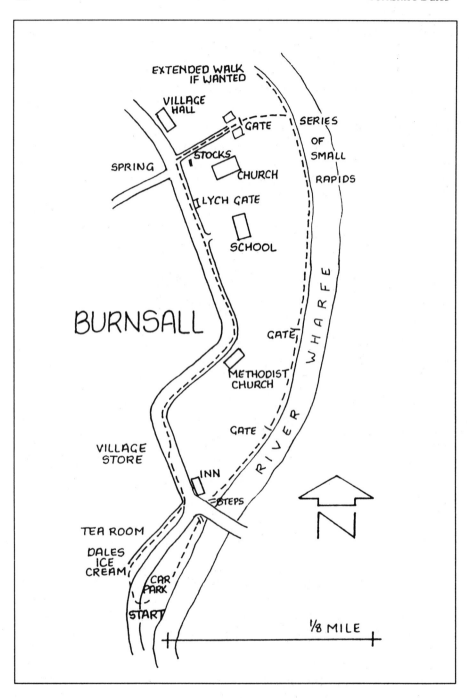

Burnsall village

river. Were the whole area rebuilt today, the reverse would almost certainly apply. One small field has a nanny goat and two small ponies stabled there.

¤ Past a kissing gate, the previously smooth water becomes some-what broken as rapids are reached. The path also gets a little more difficult underfoot.

¤ But not for long. Above the rapids, a track leaves to the left up a slight incline, passes through a gate and between a house and garage. This footpath leads back to the road.

For those wishing to savour the delights of the Wharfe a little longer, the path continues waterside as the river cuts through a somewhat rocky formation. This is a particularly attractive reach and can be extended almost ad infinitum, returning to the same point when ready.

¤ On reaching the main road, turn left and walk down the road, through the village centre and back to the car park.

¤ On reaching the road, a few metres to the right is a rather elegant

village hall, whilst across the road is the site of an old spring. Along
the road, on the left is the parish church of St Wilfrid's.

This appealing building is dedicated to St Wilfrid of Ripon (634 –
709). The church was founded by the de Romily family early in the
twelfth century on the site of a wooden Anglo-Saxon church. It was
rebuilt in the fifteenth century but much of the original beauty was
left untouched. This particularly applied to a sculptured alabaster
panel depicting the Adoration of the Magi.

A tower was added during the 1500s and further rebuilding and
development took place early the following century, creating a building very much in the Perpendicular style. Funds for this "...repair and
butification..." were provided by Sir William Craven in 1612. Further
details of this most respected of local gentlemen will be discovered
in the section devoted to Appletreewick, later in this Trail.

Further work was carried out in 1859. "Restorations" of the Victorian
era were notorious and many a wonderful church building was
visually ruined. St Wilfrid's was fortunate: it lost only the battlements
and original chancel arch.

Inside are some really ancient treasures – not of much intrinsic value,
but historically fascinating. Danish hog-back tombs, a font with
Danish markings and symbols, dated variously between 1050 and
1100.

A board at the rear describes a peculiar condition that obtained here
for six hundred years: there were two Livings. The rectors from 1270
– the first pair being John de Kyrkeby and William De Reddemere –
were appointed by respective patrons until 1876. Then the parish was
divided into Burnsall and Rylston-with-Coniston. Only then was St
Wilfrid's served by one rector.

One charming result of this historical accident is that, although the
rectors were organised, those responsible never considered the
churchwardens. Consequently, there are still four in office rather
than the standard two.

Outside in the churchyard are located the village stocks, a Celtic cross
commemorating those who died in the war and a quite ancient sun
dial amidst numerous table tombs. A peculiar lych gate is also worthy
of study. Centrally pivoted, it swings though almost 180°, closing via
a concealed counterweight, the rope to which runs over an ancient
wooden pulley.

Next door to the church is a school. This was funded – again – by Sir William Craven and was opened in 1602 as a grammar school, a function it served until 1876. It's in use to this very day, now educating primary-age children.

Burnsall Methodist Chapel dating from 1901 is on this side of the village and, approaching the centre – if it can be called such – the incidence of delightful housing increases.

Manor Cottage is one of a row which is next door to the Manor House – now offering bed and breakfast. Whichever way you look, there are the nooks and crannies of village life that repay the curious in spades.

Close By

The village of Appletreewick is a "must" for those who appreciate English villages at their finest. Mentioned in Domesday, the land here used to be owned by Bolton Priory – see Trail 1. It was when that priory was still in use that Appletreewick prospered. It was also the scene of a long-running feud between the Clifford family, who had gained possession of most of this land after the Reformation, and Sir John Yorke of Appletreewick who led a band of marauders to hunt deer on Clifford land. This conflict climaxed at Appletreewick Fair in 1621 when a huge brawl between the opposing factions took place.

Sir William Craven was a prominent local benefactor, born in poverty in a cottage across from High Hall which, along with the one next door was converted into a chapel-of-ease in 1897. Seeking an escape from penury, he went to London where he did a "Dick Whittington" in 1610 by becoming Lord Mayor of London. His largesse is evident to this day and his name honoured by The Craven Arms pub in the village.

Lead was worked, on a very ad hoc basis, throughout the middle ages and into the nineteenth century. The hills around were a good source, but without really concentrated seams. After trade finally died, it brought much poverty to the village.

Three halls still exist in Appletreewick. Monks Hall was built in 1697 on the site of the priory's grange and incorporated some of the original building. High Hall, built in Tudor style was restored by Craven. Low Hall was restored in 1658 and was for many years the home of a particularly aggressive ghost.

Trail 4: Linton-in-Craven

L inton is often called "The Prettiest Village in Wharfedale." This Trail give you the opportunity to judge for yourself.

Trail Facts

Distance:	2½ miles
Clean Shoe Rating:	9
Map:	O.S. Landranger Series No 98
Start:	Riverside car park north of Linton
Starting Grid Ref:	SE 002631
Car Parking:	See above
Refreshment:	Pub in Linton-in-Craven
Nearest TIC	National Parks Centre, Hebden Road, Grassington, N. York-shire BD23 5LB – 01756 752748.

¤ Leave the car park heading left (away from the toilet block). After only a couple of hundred metres there is a decision to be made. Off to the right, a track leads down to Linton Falls.

An attractive area of the river, there used to be a textile mill until it closed in 1959. Even before then, it had a chequered history. Over the centuries, there have been mills on this site, first grinding corn, then spinning worsteds before a spell as a cotton mill.

¤ After visiting the falls, return to the route. Walk up the road to a junction and carry straight on. This eventually reaches a cross-roads: again, straight on. On the brow of the hill is a building marked: *The Arthur Anderton Memorial Institute And Men's Reading Room.*

¤ Soon, Linton is reached. Just before the road bridge, the house set back on the right is White Abbey.

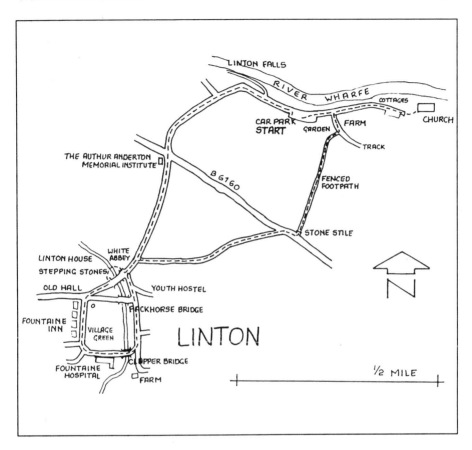

This seventeenth-century house was never used for church purposes, it was always as it is today.

¤ You now have to get to the other side of Linton Beck. Perhaps the most fun way – if the river is not carrying too much water – is to turn right now, walk diagonally across the field towards the stepping stones and across that way. On reaching the other side, turn left towards the green.

The Manor House on the corner just beyond the bridge is a century or so older than most of the houses in this village. Linton Beck is the central feature, with several crossings. There's a clapper or packhorse bridge, ford, stepping stones – in fact pretty well every way to cross water is used here.

The elegant bridge spanning the Wharfe at Linton

An unusual monument on the village green is surmounted by a gyroscope. It's: "A Tribute to Linton-in-Craven on Being Adjudged First in the News Chronicle Loveliest Village in the North Competition 1949." As it's now well over thirty years since that daily paper disappeared from our streets, the village is unlikely to win again.

The seventeenth-century Fountaine Inn has a super collection of beers available and also serves food. Opening hours are: 12 noon to 2.30pm and 7pm to 10.30pm, closed Sunday evenings and Mondays – except Bank holidays.

There are several delightful side streets leading off the green to the right. Explore them by all means – you'll be delighted at what you see, but they all return to the green. At the far end of here is the Grade II Listed Fountaine Hospital.

This was endowed by Richard Fountaine in 1721. It's not a hospital within the meaning of the Act, but a series of almshouses in an elegant classical building of a type quite unknown previously in the Dales.

There is a theory that it was designed by Sir John Vanbrugh, the eminent architect and playwright. He was the man responsible for

Castle Howard nearby and Blenheim Palace in Oxfordshire. The connection? Fountaine was his timber merchant in charge of selecting wood for the great man's work.

The chapel attached has only recently (1994) been restored to use. It's usually open for visitors and, whilst spartan, is still worthy of a visit.

¤ Cross back over the river. Exactly how you do that is your choice. The nearest crossing to the chapel is a clapper bridge which used to be sited north of the road where the stepping stones now are. It was moved when the main road bridge was installed in 1892.

A little lower, and centrepiece of the scene here is the fourteenth-century packhorse bridge. Alongside, there is a ford – should you dare.

¤ Walk back out of the village along the road you came in on for a few metres, then take the narrow lane bearing right. At the end, bear right again and after 100 metres, a stone stile leads off to the left.

¤ This well-surfaced path, fenced off from the field, bears to the right as it drops down the hill. At the end, turn left to the road and then right. This runs alongside the river and gives access to the church.

The church here is St Michael and All Angels, which serves the communities of Grassington, Linton, Hebden and Threshfield. As you pass through a gate into the churchyard, you are confronted by a squat square bell tower and very plain exterior. This is scant preparation for the charming interior of the building. The earliest part dates back to around 1240, but most of the place was rebuilt during the fourteenth century. Some scholars state that there was a Saxon church on this spot, but there is no visual evidence.

¤ Return along the road you have just walked and the car park is on the left.

Trail 5: Grassington

G rassington is ancient. There is evidence of Neolithic settlement at Lea Green, north of Grassington, where old burial grounds exist. Relics discovered indicate use during the Bronze and Iron Ages, the Romans were here, and a Celtic field system can still be seen.

The name is probably derived from the Saxon pasture farm. Settlement had moved from Lea Green to this spot well before Norman times and was handed over to Norman lords after the conquest. Evidence of its importance over the centuries can be gleaned from the fact that a market Charter was granted in 1282. Since then, it has developed as the first town of Wharfedale. Its continued pre-eminence was assured after the estate passed to the Devonshires.

Lead had been worked, almost as a pastime, for centuries. Then, in the seventeenth century, work was co-ordinated by the Duke of Devonshire who also owns the glorious Chatsworth House near Bakewell (Derbyshire). This was an area strong in lead mining tradition, and altogether better organised.

The duke imported experienced miners from that area and intense production ensued. This brought relative prosperity to Grassington. Corn mills were established on the river bank. Turnpike roads were built and corn gave way to textile production. Everything in Grassington's garden was rosy.

But, bust follows boom as sure as night follows day. Cheap foreign imports (where have we heard that before?) killed the lead industry by the middle of the nineteenth century. By then, steam power was wiping out water power by its efficiency. Grassington's water-powered plant was obsolete and its owners moved away to where fuel could be more readily obtained. Grassington Moor is still riddled with old lead workings, whilst of the mills there is no trace.

Then the economic swing took a turn for the better. A railway was built from Skipton in 1901, terminating in Threshfield, just across the Wharfe. Easy transport was at last available, and the masses from the West Riding discovered this delightful valley. Tourism, albeit of the day-tripping variety hit Grassington. Although the railway lasted a relatively short time, it was there long enough to introduce the world to Wharfedale.

Today, the whole area – and Grassington in particular – continues a love/hate relationship with visitors. To have your windows peered through day and night, winter and summer, must be wearing in the extreme, but, if the area were declared a no-go for visitors, Grassington would surely ossify.

Grass Wood Nature Reserve – privately owned – just north of Grassington in the same area as Lea Green, is botanically famous for the number of uncommon plants that grow there amongst the more usual ones. Growing alongside lily-of-the-valley, you may find orchids, including some of the rarer ones, birds-eye primrose, and Jacob's Ladder. There are even a few Alpines, probably a left-over from the Ice Age.

One of the many superb stone buildings lining the square in Grassington

Trail Facts

Distance:	½ mile
Clean Shoe Rating:	10
Map:	O.S. Landranger Series No 98
Start:	Barclays Bank, at the corner of Hebden Road and Main Street.
Starting Grid Ref:	SE 004639
Car Parking:	Several on the edge of town, a few in the square.
Refreshment:	In profusion
Nearest TIC	National Parks Centre, Hebden Road, Grassington, N. Yorkshire BD23 5LB – 01756 752748.

¤   Cross Main Street and walk straight ahead into Wood Lane.

The Dales Toffee Shop has a wonderful selection of confectionery, much of it boiled in White Rose country. Just how Uncle Joe's Mint Balls (super sweets, but made in Wigan) come to be included is something of a mystery. The ice cream is also made within the county, and excellent it is too.

A few metres along Wood Lane, on the left is Grassington National School. This was built in 1844, funded by the National Society to provide schooling long before it became compulsory. It closed in 1981 and the building has been tastefully converted to housing.

¤   Take the first turning to the right, a narrow alleyway and walk to the top, bearing right to avoid the Devonshire Hotel. On reaching the road, turn left.

Walking up this alleyway, note the building on the left, behind the hedge. This is.The Old Hall, the medieval manor house, dating back to the thirteenth century. Although much modified over the years, greatly in the nineteenth century, there is enough historical interest for it to be listed Grade I. It's still in private hands and reputed to be the oldest inhabited house in Wharfedale.

¤   Walk up the hill towards the Town Hall.

Much of this area, centred around the Square is a conservation area. There are houses, shops, pubs and restaurants, all built with not the slightest consideration for what today is known as a building line.

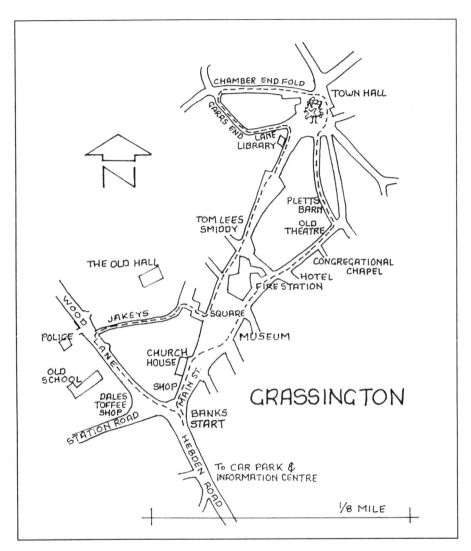

That we will never re-create the glorious untidiness of a village like this that our descendants could admire will be a cross placed firmly at the door of our town planners. Their slavish adherence to formulae, supine acceptance of "current practice" and fear of anything even slightly out of the ordinary is very sad.

On this section of Main Street you will find a butcher who sells high quality meat, traditionally presented. How many places today will slice bacon from the joint in the exact thickness you want? No pre-packed, water-filled taste-free offering here. Sausages too. Full and meaty: real "bangers".

Note Martyn Fretwell's Shenstone Gallery on the left. This is the original Old Smidy where blacksmith Tom Lee worked in 1766. Then he murdered a local doctor, a crime for which he was executed in York, his body being returned to Grass Woods where it was hung in chains.

The Dales Kitchen, one of the eating establishments offers a series of gourmet evenings where cuisine from a selected country around the world is on offer. It's also Egon Ronay recommended.

¤   At the top, turn left into Garrs End Lane. Walk along here, around a right-hand bend, and before the next road is met, turn sharp right, up a cobbled ramp into (un-named) Chamber End Fold.

This charming area was once occupied by the lead miners. The housing is ancient and, again, totally lacks even a hint of conformity.

¤   At the end, walk straight across, past the tree. After 75 metres, there is three way split. Take the right-hand fork – Water Lane but un-marked – made of deteriorating cobble and at the end, turn right, downhill.

The Town Hall has its origins as a Mechanics Institute with funds provided by the Duke of Devonshire. At the end of the last century, it was extended and re-named to mark the duke's munificence.

Pletts Barn, on the right of Water Lane was once just that. The seventeenth-century Listed building has been skilfully converted to an outdoor supplies shop. Evidence of its original use is easy to discover. Note particularly the slits to the right of the main wall, just beyond the shop window. This was the dovecote.

Although we tend to regard pigeons as vermin today, they were a carefully grown crop until this century when better meat became more generally available. Farms and most houses of any note had their own dovecotes, providing meat throughout the year.

¤   Walk back down the hill, through the Square and to the road junction at the bottom where this Trail started.

On the left is Grassington Congregational Church, gaunt and very much at odds with its surroundings. This started life in 1811 as a Methodist Chapel when non-conformist religion featured greatly in the lives of working men and women. It was probably built as a direct result of the Derbyshire miners arriving here.

Opposite, a house called Theatre Cottage. Converted from a barn, it was a thriving theatre in the last century. Lower down, on the right, an unprepossessing shed houses the Grassington Volunteer Fire Service. With the nearest council fire station some miles away, the town maintains this delightful anachronism to help out in emergencies: very efficient it is too.

To the left of the Square is Upper Wharfedale Museum, a fine exposition of life hereabouts as it has been over the centuries. Much thought, effort and time have been expended to make this display, staffed by volunteers: what a shame it's only open from 2pm to 4pm.

At the foot of the Square, to the right is Church House. The datestone is inscribed 1694. With Georgian windows above, it was a family home for years, owned by a succession of businessmen. Today, it serves the town in a variety of ways, being now owned by the church.

This simply superb building is a fine way to round off this tour of Grassington. But there is much, much more to find: given the time. Exploring the multitude of Folds and Alleys can be a rewarding experience.

One final point. Each June, Grassington holds a Festival. Spread over two weeks, it's a popular event, attracting some quite well-known names. Recent years have seen Barry Cryer, Willie Rushton, Brian Blessed and The Temperance Seven – not bad for such a small place. At the festival, there's music, usually including a top quality brass band and recitals, humour and poetry. The Information Centre will have details of this year's programme.

Trail 6: Kettlewell

This charming little village is history personified. It nestles into a steep valley where Park Gill Beck joins the Wharfe, steep hills all around, with Great Whernside (2310ft/704m) standing, forbiddingly, over the lot. It was in this area that the earliest recorded inhabitants of these Dales, the Brigantes, gathered. These people came originally from an area around the German/Austrian/Swiss border, crossing the Channel long before the Romans. They were men of the hills with skills in animal husbandry.

Their queen co-operated with the Romans when they appeared on the scene. This did not suit her husband Venutius who left her to form a large army of dissidents. Their base was at Ingleborough. From there they continued to harass the Romans.

Now, Romans were not keen on being harassed. Realising that they would march to sort him out, Venutius built a series of fortifications. One, a ditch and rampart, was built above Kettlewell. But resistance was futile; Venutius and his followers were routed and Roman rule enforced.

But, with a bloody-mindedness that was to become a trait in Yorkshiremen, sporadic outbreaks of violence and mayhem were perpetrated by dissenting locals. It needed a large army together with a network of good roads to keep the Dales subjugated.

At the time of Domesday, there was a thriving settlement in Kettlewell. The influence of Fountains Abbey was felt here as, together with Bolton and Coverham, they had use of the land. It was managed as a vast sheep estate. A Market Charter was granted in 1320 and livestock were sold there at both weekly gatherings and the huge Autumn Fairs.

In common with other villages in the Wharfedale area, lead mining was carried out on the hills. Again, miners came to live and work in the village causing a population explosion that stretched the village to its limits.

It was also on the edge of two great hunting forests, Langstrough-dale and Littondale. After the Dissolution, the estates were gradually broken up and the yeoman farmer found wealth and freedom. This accounts for much of the building that took place around that time.

A blow to the prestige of the village was struck when the railway, heading north from Skipton, terminated near Grassington. This left Kettlewell distinctly second best. But with the growth of motor transport, increasing numbers of people have discovered this delight-ful village and on summer weekends and in high season, it's as busy as elsewhere. But this popularity has not obscured the great beauty of Kettlewell. The whole village is a conservation area.

Kilnsey Crags, south of the village are a mecca for rock climbers. There is usually a group of energetic young people to be seen, doing their impersonations of flies. Kilnsey Park is a series of attractions offering the visitor a chance to fish for trout, visit the "Daleslife" visitor centre or the farm shop. An adventure playground keeps youngsters happy.

The stocks at Kettlewell

Trail Facts

Distance:	1 mile
Clean Shoe Rating:	6 when wet, 10 when dry
Map:	O.S. Landranger Series No 98
Start:	Kettlewell village car park, by the B6160 alongside the Wharfe.
Starting Grid Ref:	SD 968723
Car Parking:	As above
Refreshment:	Plenty all around the start/finish
Nearest TIC	National Parks Centre, Hebden Road, Grassington, N. Yorkshire BD23 5LB

¤ Leave the car park and turn left. Almost immediately, there is a right turn at The Old Smithy, now a gift shop.

The Cottage Tea Room offers a splendid range of food, from a pot of tea to quite elaborate menus. Quality – and quantity – is excellent and, if you are looking for somewhere to stay, the owners Mike and Jaynie Smith can offer you rooms with four-poster beds, whirlpool baths, country views and the amazing "As-much-as-you-can-eat" Great Yorkshire Breakfast: also known as a heart attack on a plate. Rooms are very reasonably priced: details on 01756 760405.

¤ Carry on along this road with Park Gill Beck to the left, Low Hall on the right, now an outdoor equipment shop. The village stocks are still on display to the left by the war memorial. At the next junction, bear left, alongside the maypole. This was re-erected by Kettlewell Women's Institute to commemorate the Coronation of Queen Elizabeth II on June 2nd 1953.

¤ A short way along this road is The Kings Head, a free house. Turn right here to visit the church of St Mary.

Remarkably, this archetypal Dales church with low chunky tower is not yet 200 years old, the rebuild of a twelfth-century one. Sadly, the only remaining artefact from that church is the curious tub shaped font which is of Norman origin. The lych gate is also new, erected in 1921 by the then vicar. One of our minor novelists, C.J. Cutcliff Hyne lived in the village and is buried in the churchyard.

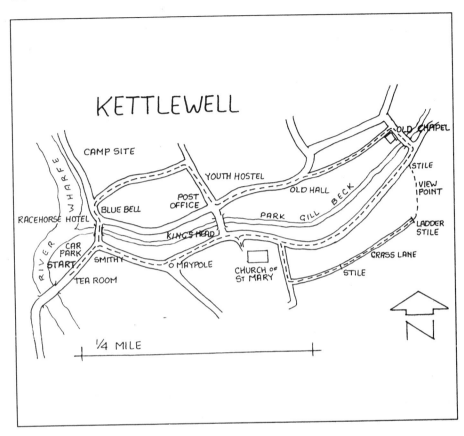

Back to the road, on the corner by the Kings Head, a cast iron marker will be seen. The letters "WR" cast into it indicate that when Yorkshire was a "proper" county with three ridings, the beck formed the dividing line between North and West ridings.

¤ Take the road that carries on up alongside the beck, rather than crossing the bridge.

¤ At the first right, a decision has to be made. By far the most scenic view is gained by turning right. It also involves unmade tracks, stiles and fields. This section affects the "Clean Shoe" rating: if this concerns you, carry straight on up the gentle hill and rejoin the Trail at *.

¤ Take the first right alongside some very nice housing and turn first

left, along the back of them. Over a stile into a narrow lane with dry
stone walling to either side. Climb the ladder stile at the end of this
section and turn left.

This is certainly the place to pause awhile and look back over the
valley towards the scree-covered sheer slopes of Gate Cote Scar.

¤   Go through an opening to the next stile. This leads into the lane;
turn right.

¤   * Immediately to the left is a narrow bridge over the beck. Take this,
pass the old Methodist chapel (1860) on the left, now converted to
residential use and turn left alongside, between that building and
a house called Fellfoot. This narrow track heads back down the
other side of the beck.

¤   Rejoin a road, pass Old Hall and several other houses of quite aged
appearance. Over the doors of these – and many others like them
– a datestone will be found. Together with the date, there are
usually three initials carved. The centre one of these indicated the
surname of the owner, the left-hand one is the husband's first
name, the right-hand one, that of the wife.

¤   At the next road junction, with the village post office and stores
across, turn right. Follow this around to the left, past a series of
ancient houses to eventually arrive at the main road.

Hard left is The Blue Bell Hotel which is a residential free house,
across the way, The Racehorses Hotel. Both serve fine Yorkshire beer
and good food: take your pick.

¤   Take the half left, over the bridge and bear right with the road, back
to the car park.

Trail 7: Arncliffe

Another village nestling in a valley, this time in Littondale. Arncliffe is one of those out of the way places with roads to it, but not going to many places beyond. That notwithstanding, in recent years the place has been known to get quite busy during the holidays season and at weekends during much of the year.

Trail Facts

Distance:	½ mile
Clean Shoe Rating:	10
Map:	O.S. Landranger Series No 98
Start:	Arncliffe Square
Starting Grid Ref:	SD932718
Car Parking:	Roadside in the square
Refreshment:	Tea room and pub
Nearest TIC	National Parks Centre, Hebden Road, Grassington, N. Yorkshire BD23 5LB – 01756 752748.

¤   Being such a small village, the Trail around it will be in the form of a figure-of-eight. That way, it is possible to take in everything there is to see.

The houses and farms surrounding the green are probably a relic of successive Scandinavian invaders who settled here during the dark ages. They were given to creating large greens in the centre of their settlements where livestock could be safely left overnight. One barn to the north has a porched entrance with a 1677 datestone. Old Cotes is a charming residence from 1650 with gabled porch and three light windows. There is much, much more to be seen by diligent exploration.

¤   Leave the green taking a narrow lane to the north, left of the post

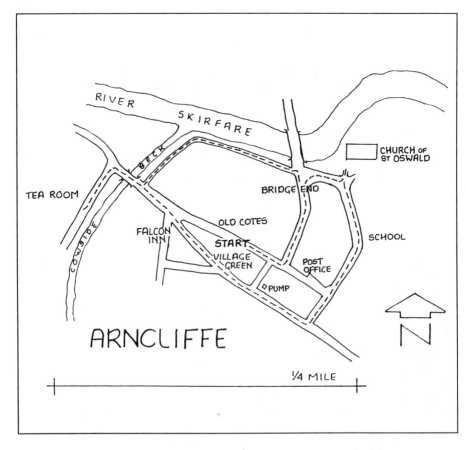

office, the entrance to which is cunningly concealed in a recess.
This narrow lane descends gently towards the river.

A house near the bridge, surprisingly (!) called "Bridge End" was once
owned by the Hammond family. Charles Kingsley, the author, stayed
in the house with the family. He was so captivated by the place that
when he came to write his marvellous children's book "The Water
Babies", the house and hostess were fictionalised and incorporated
into the story.

And, not content with that, the valley itself was used as the setting
for the book, under the name of "Vendale". Although a man of Devon,
Kingsley knew, loved and indeed worked in this area for some of his

life. He is also very well known for that west country saga "Westward Ho!"

And, for further literary connection in this sweet valley, William Wordsworth was another who visited the dale. He also incorporated it into his work, this time under the fictitious name of the "deep fork of Amerdale."

Then to bring the "literary" (using the word in its loosest possible context) connections up to date, Yorkshire Television have used the immediate area in recent years as location settings for their long-running "soap", "Emmerdale Farm".

¤   At the bottom, turn right.

The twelfth-century church of St Oswald is on the left. This has been restored to such a degree that most of its interest has been lost. The major work was carried out in 1796, with more in 1841. Its squat, square tower, so thoroughly in keeping with the Dales scenery, is all that remains from the original building of about 1500. Three bells hang up there, the oldest c1350. Inside, a scroll gives the names (and accoutrements) of local dalesmen who fought at Flodden Field in 1513. Otherwise, the greatest antiquity is hidden: in that very tower.

The Scots were persistent raiders into this area, causing dislocation of life far in excess of their numbers. Henry, the Shepherd Lord Clifford assembled and led a band of his tenants to Flodden, and it was he and his men who, when the Scots under James IV and assisted by the French, looked as though they may triumph, led a counter-attack that saw a wavering English line surge to overwhelming triumph. The death of James and many of his followers then ensured a cessation of hostilities for almost half a century.

¤   Walk up the hill past the tiny schoolroom.

It is a delight to see that it is still possible to achieve education in rural areas such as this. Too many places have lost their schools with pupils having to travel long distances to be educated. The economics are irresistible, but the quality of education handed out by these places is so much more convincing.

¤   At the top, turn right, walk along the street, past the green, a pub

An old well in Arncliffe

called the Falcon on the left and straight ahead to a bridge. Just
before this turn right.

On the bridge is a cast metal plate warning that the bridge will not
carry traction engines and other vehicles of excess size. This was
produced by Settle Rural District Council. A small but pleasant
diversion can be made. Cross over the bridge, turn left, and a tea room
will be discovered a little way along the road.

¤ Walk alongside Cowside Beck for some 200 metres until the
confluence of that water and the river Skirfare is reached.

Eventually, this will flow into the Wharfe. In this exquisite valley,
thought by many to be the most beautiful of the dales, primroses and
daffodils grow wild and in profusion. Needless to say, springtime is
when it appears in all its finery.

¤ Turn right alongside the river and follow this track until it reaches
the river bridge. This is worth a few metres detour to examine more
closely. Then, turn right back up the hill towards the village green.

Trail 8: Malham

To take in all the wonders of the Malham area is beyond the scope of this book. Sitting astride the Pennine Way, Malham – as a village – is unremarkable, at least by the standards of what has gone before. But, in the context of scenery around, it is a magnet to visitors from all over the world.

Approaching from the south, through Kirkby Malham, alongside the infant river Aire must be one of the more dramatic drives in England. The crescent of rugged limestone crags that fills the windscreen takes the breath away.

There is a classic walk – arguably one of the finest in England – which takes in the Tarn, Malham Cove and Janet's Foss. Our Trail will be less adventurous but equally absorbing, without the thrombosis-inducing climb/scramble around Gordale Scar.

Malham Tarn

Trail Facts

Distance:	2 miles: shorter version, 1 mile
Clean Shoe Rating:	Short version – 8: Full length – 2
Map:	O.S. Landranger Series No 98
Start:	National Park Centre, Malham
Starting Grid Ref:	SD 900627
Car Parking:	At the centre
Refreshment:	All in the village
Nearest TIC	National Park Centre, Malham, North Yorkshire – 01729 830363

¤ Leave the centre and turn left, into Malham. At the first junction, bear right over the beck.

The first building is a somewhat unprepossessing Methodist chapel on the left. But from there, things improve as ancient building follows ancient building. Again, datestones over doorways stand mute testimony to their history.

A blacksmith still carries on his trade at a small smithy to the right. Sadly, no horses will be tied up, having new shoes fitted; his work today is mainly decorative ironwork. There is a tea room to the left, followed by The Buck Inn.

¤ Walk past the Lister Arms hotel on the left, Malham Cafe on the right, and the YHA on the left. Keep along this road until the first real road on the left leaves for "Malham Tarn – 3 miles. Take this and bear left again onto a stoned track after 100 metres.

¤ Pass The Old School and, when the track divides in front of the first housing, bear right, keeping to the good track. Soon, this turns sharp right into King House, whilst the Trail continues directly ahead along a road of somewhat lesser quality. At the end of this section is a "T" junction.

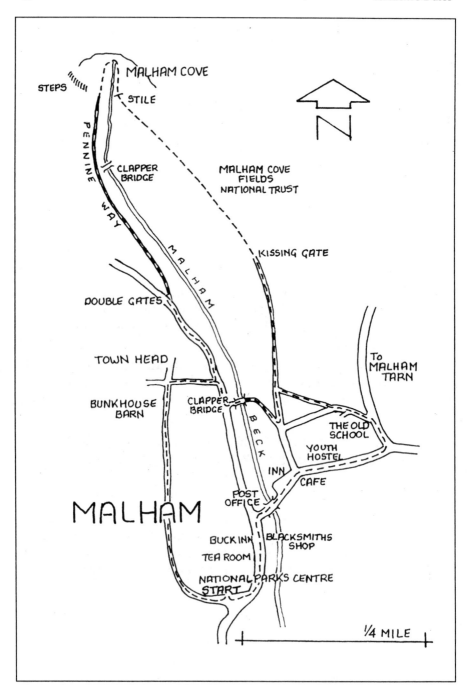

Shorter Trail

¤ Turn left here, walk down the lane for 75 yards and take the right-hand turn that almost doubles back on itself, down to the river, over the bridge/ford to the road. Turn right and walk up here to Townhead. On the right is a sign: KMPC ATKINSON COPSE. Turn left here, up the public footpath and pick up the Trail description at
*

Full Length Trail

¤ Turn right at this point, up the lane and through a kissing gate on to Malham Cove Fields, National Trust property. This follows a clearly marked track, ever closer to the wonderful rock formation that is Malham Cove.

This unique exposure of the Mid-Craven fault stands 262ft (80m) high and is some 985ft (300m) across. Once, after the Ice Age, the outflow from Malham Tarn flowed over the face and must have created a most spectacular waterfall. The erosion from this also helps explain the concave shape we see today.

Only after exceptionally heavy rainfall can this waterfall be seen in action; even then, it's a mere trickle, the water windblown long before it hits the bottom. The ledges along the face of the Cove are created by variations in the hardness of the limestone, vertical linings visible are actually mosses growing on the face.

Since those days, the Tarn outflow has found an underground route that sees it surface south of Malham as a spring at Aire Head. The water running down from the foot of the Cove comes from a sink to the north west, high on the moor; all part of the convoluted system of caves, underground rivers and potholes that riddle these hills.

¤ Follow the clearly marked path. This gradually converges with the water, but there is no way across; save paddling. Walk almost to the foot of the cliff before the spring bubbling up from under huge boulders allows a crossing to the other side. Take care here, some of these rocks are very slippery. Across the other side, make for the path and walk back down the beck.

¤ Close to, this Cove looks even more impressive. To the left is a path which leads into a flight of steps, finally to the summit of this great crag. The view from up there is sensational, but a huge amount of "puff" will be expended getting there. Is it worth it? You bet!

This, and some of our return Trail is actually a section of The Pennine Way. Britain's very first long distance footpath – and probably the finest – was established in 1965. Its history can be traced back to the National Parks Act of 1949. This set up a National Parks Commission (now The Countryside Commission) who had the power to create these paths. Starting at Edale in Derbyshire, it makes its way north along the roof of England for 270 miles (334km) and over the border into Scotland to Kirk Yetholm.

¤   Continue down the clearly marked, and well-surfaced, path to a double gate that leads to a road. Turn left and walk downhill.

Over on the eastern slopes of this valley, lynchets can be seen. These terraces, created to make cultivation of the land easier, were developed by Anglian farmers in the seventh century.

Down in the valley, there once stood a mill. In the thirteenth century it was owned by the monks of Fountains Abbey. They rented it out and corn was ground there. The income generated from rent was used to alleviate poverty.

Looking back towards the Cove, the large field to the left, the one with lots of ridges in it, was in use as an Iron Age settlement in the third century BC.

¤   Around a couple of bends and a track bears off to the right with a sign offering bunkhouse accommodation on the corner. A hundred yards further along, a footpath sign points to the right, towards Townhead. This is the Trail.

¤   * At the top of this path, turn left and continue down the lane. All too soon, the car park comes into view on the left. The path swings to the left to reach the entrance gate.

Trail 9: Gargrave

A small village sitting astride the busy A65 road from the West Riding to Cumbria, Gargrave may soon be a far more pleasant place than it sometimes is today. That road is the reason; and a projected bypass the solution.

Trail Facts

Distance:	2 miles
Clean Shoe Rating:	8
Map:	O.S. Landranger Series No 103
Start:	North Street Car Park, Gargrave.
Starting Grid Ref:	SD 933543
Car Parking:	See above
Refreshment:	Several pubs and a cafe in the village, none very far away.
Nearest TIC	9 Sheep Street, Skipton, N. Yorkshire, BD23 1JH – 01756 792809.

¤ Across the road is Gargrave Village Hall. Take the road that will take you to the right of that building. This is West Street, although there is no name plate at this end.

¤ There is an alternative car park a few metres along this walk, on the right-hand side.

¤ This leads to the main road. Cross and turn right. Walk along the road to the speed derestriction signs. There, a gap in the railings to the left gives access to a set of stepping stones over the river Aire.

The river, which rose quite close to Malham, visited on Trail 8, flows generally to the east. It is responsible for the huge valley from here towards Leeds. Beyond that city, it becomes navigable in section until it finally empties into the river Ouse near Goole.

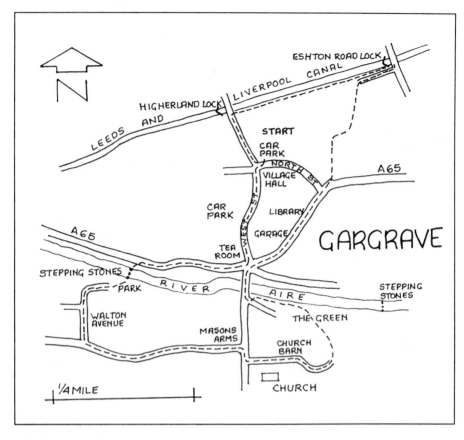

Whilst walking along this road, examine some of the houses across the way. Although somewhat faded grandeur may be the term that best describes them, there is still a good amount of fine construction to be seen. Again, when the thundering lorries have left their front doors alone, a degree of gentility may again return.

¤ Cross the stepping stones and at the far side bear half right across the park. At the end, join a macadam path which leads to a road. Turn left.

¤ Walk along Walton Avenue, up the rise to the top and turn left. Follow this road, past several grand old mansions to the junction at the end. The Masons Arms stands on the left-hand corner. Turn right and enter the church yard.

Church Gates Farmhouse, with attractive Dales-style window frames is on the corner. It appears to be of some antiquity, it was only built in 1903. Next door, the Church Barn, now converted to live in is a venerable old building, dated 1670.

The church is one of the less interesting ones visited during the course of this book, but in the south east corner, beneath a large cross, lie the mortal remains of Iain Norman MacLeod. He was a Member of Parliament, Privy Councillor and a crucial part of the Heath government when he died on July 20th 1970. He had been appointed Chancellor of the Exchequer only a few weeks when his death stunned the political world. He was a Yorkshireman, born in Skipton on November 11th 1913.

Lined neatly around the graveyard perimeter are a series of very ancient tombstones: 1715 and 1634 are two of the more prominent ones. One, noting the death of a gentleman aged forty-one, has the 'four' carved in mirror image.

¤ Continue down Church lane until the road drops down a little dip. Here, bear left with the road, beyond a row of houses, back to the river. Turn left, and continue alongside the water to the bridge. Leave the river, cross the bridge and turn right. Walk down the main road.

Note the ancient garage on the left. From here Pennine Motors have provided motor coaches for decades. A look at the front will convey something of the timeless nature of this place. The front entrance, apart from being too low and narrow for modern buses, would create an enormous traffic hazard were their coaches to reverse into the street today. A few metres further along, over the wall, the current depot can be seen.

¤ Where the main road turns sharp right just beyond the post office, another road leaves to the left. Almost on the intersection, across the road, is a narrow path, best identified by the "No Cycling" boards. Walk along here, past a couple of kissing gates, and eventually to the canal; but with a stone wall between. At the end of the path, double back along the canal towing path beside Eshton Road lock.

A flower-garlanded stone building in Gargrave

To the right, just out of sight along the canal is another lock. This, at Holme Bridge, marks the start of a quite remarkable seventeen miles of canal before the huge five-rise locks at Bingley. Looking at the mountainous terrain all around, the achievements of those surveyors over two centuries ago is quite astonishing.

¤   Walk along the canal towing path to the next bridge. Here, turn left by another – Higherland – lock and walk down the road. The car park is on the left at the bottom.

Trail 10: Settle

In the short distance between Malham (Trail 9) and Settle, the Pennines have created a watershed. All rivers so far in this book eventually flowed into the North Sea. From Settle, the Ribble heads west to the Irish sea. A bridge over the river, built in Tudor times, saw Settle as the focal point for travellers between Yorkshire and Westmoreland. Settle has had a market since 1249, the Charter being granted by Henry III, and it still flourishes today, albeit somewhat changed in form.

The town is compact, has a fine collection of old buildings and pubs, many dating back some three hundred years. In recent years, the opening of a bypass has restored a degree of sanity to Settle. It had become a nightmare of a place: trying to cross the road in summer was an exercise in patience.

Something over a hundred years ago, a railway connection with Carlisle was built. This has achieved a degree of fame in recent years as the Settle and Carlisle railway, the most spectacular in England.

Today, much of Settle's economy is tourist based. Being centrally placed around the three peaks of Pen-y-ghent, Ingleborough and Whernside.

Trail Facts

Distance:	1 mile
Clean Shoe Rating:	10
Map:	O.S. Landranger Series No 98
Start:	Market Square, Settle
Starting Grid Ref:	SD 820636
Car Parking:	Several parks around the town and in the market square
Refreshment:	Pubs and cafes in the centre
Nearest TIC	Cheapside, Settle, North Yorkshire BD24 9EJ – 01729 825192.

¤ From the Market Square, cross the road and take the narrow lane to the left of The Old Naked Man cafe.

On the right-hand building, above the ground floor is the said gentleman. To avoid an arrest for obscenity, the man holds a plaque approximately the shape of a pair of underpants. On this is the date.

¤ Walk down this narrow cobbled street, noting the seventeenth-century Bishopdale House on the right. On reaching a hairdressers on the right, bear left to the "proper" road and turn right along it, under the railway before turning left.

Niceties observed for The Old Naked Man

This road was the original, leading towards Kendal via a ford over the Ribble. It was also the main road into Giggleswick. Until 1837, Settle had no parish church and people from this side had to cross the river to Giggleswick for services.

A building on the left used to be the Spread Eagle Inn. Now it's a private house carrying a blue plaque on the wall. Here, the well-known painter Thomas Proctor (1753-1794) was born. Across the road, the Society of Friends have their Meeting House. This dates from 1689. Then, hard by the railway bridge, The Victoria Hall. This was a music hall in 1853. Still in use today, though sadly, no music hall; just concerts and plays.

¤ Walk along Bond Lane, already out on the edge of Settle. At the next junction, turn hard left and note Rose Cottage controlling the

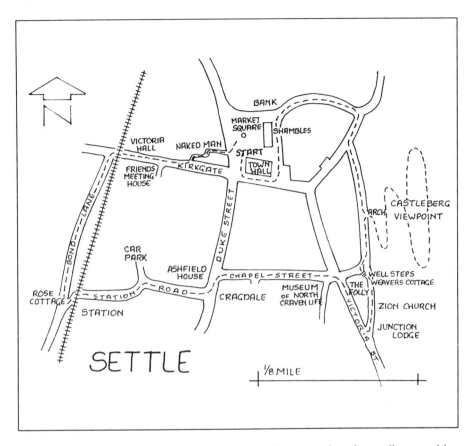

BANK

MARKET SQUARE ○ SHAMBLES

VICTORIA HALL NAKED MAN

START

FRIENDS MEETING HOUSE KIRKGATE

TOWN HALL

CASTLEBERG ARCH VIEWPOINT

CAR PARK

ASHFIELD HOUSE

CHAPEL — STREET

WELL STEPS WEAVERS COTTAGE

ROSE COTTAGE

STATION

CRAGDALE

MUSEUM OF NORTH CRAVEN LIFE

THE FOLLY

ZION CHURCH

STATION

JUNCTION LODGE

SETTLE

⅛ MILE

junction, an intriguing old building. Pass under the railway with Settle station to the right. A house alongside the station has a pagoda-like building in the garden with huge wind chimes that sound quite delightful.

If common sense had prevailed over pride, the railway line to Carlisle would never have been built and Settle would have remained a sleepy little backwater whose only connection to the outside world would have been the A65 trunk road from the West Riding to Kendal; and the Lake District.

In the 1860s, the Midland Railway Company was anxious to get its share of lucrative trade between England and Scotland. They approached the London and North Western Railway about a joint agreement and were rebuffed.

The only answer then was to build a line for themselves. They already had a station – St Pancras – in London and a link with Lancaster from Leeds. An agreement with the Glasgow and South western company ensured access to their station in Glasgow via Dumfries and Kilmarnock.

In 1869, construction of the railway began. It would start two miles south of Settle, diverging from the Lancaster line and head up the Ribble valley over some of the bleakest country in England before picking up the Eden valley for a long descent to Petteril Bridge Junction, on the edge of Carlisle. The statistics are awe-inspiring. A few metres short of 73 miles (117km), it climbed towards the summit at Ais Gill for over twenty miles at a ruling gradient of 1: 100. This became known to generations of steam engine crews as "The Long Drag" and firemen toiled to keep the steam coming. At the summit, it is 1145ft (349m) above sea level. Of tunnels there are many. The longest is 2629 metres at Blea Moor, burrowing some 500ft (152m) under the hills.

The work was long and arduous. Some 6,000 navvies were employed on the work and some lost their lives. The remains of over a hundred workers and camp followers are buried in the churchyard at Chapel-le-Dale, west of Ribblehead. Not that all lost their lives in the construction. This was authentic frontierland. The wild Pennine weather and wild navvies made wilder by drink created a heavy toll in both life and human misery.

Contemporary reports of the conditions defy comprehension today. Navvies were housed in camps alongside the work. One, at Batty Green near Ribblehead had over 2,000 workers living in squalor. The Manchester City Mission were present, as were Methodist ministers, but they fought an uphill battle against drink and prostitution. Smallpox struck during 1871, claiming many victims. Dalesmen breathed a collective sigh of relief when the line finally opened in 1876 and these navvies moved on.

Services were inaugurated between London's St Pancras station and St Enoch in Glasgow. They were fast – the MR being noted for its lightweight engines and trains. The Thames Clyde Express ran for many a decade, linking the two cities and a train from London to Edinburgh over the Settle/Carlisle section became known as the Thames Forth Express.

The contraction of Britain's railway system after the Beeching report inevitably affected the Settle line. In 1970, all the intermediate stations except Appleby were closed. Within a few years, noises demanding re-opening were being heard. Although BR took little notice, elected local bodies did. Lancashire and Cumbria councils joined with the Countryside Commission, the Yorkshire Dales National Parks Committee and the West Yorkshire Passenger Transport Executive to create "Dalesrail". This offered out-and-back day excursions from towns and cities in both Lancashire and Yorkshire to the closed stations on the line, bringing a degree of relief to hard pressed local roads.

There have been several attempts to close the line completely. The last, in the 1980s, created a huge furore, not only from the few locals who used it but, literally, from around the world. It revolved around the state of Ribblehead viaduct. Some 440 yards long and 100ft (30.5m) high, the searching winds, perennially howling up the valley, brought about imminent danger of collapse: according to British Rail engineers. They said repairs would cost millions, totally unjustified expenditure, closure was the only option.

"Rubbish!" Said a determined band who engaged their own engineers to examine the problem. They reported that only a fraction of the railways estimate was needed. Meanwhile, track over the viaduct had been singled as the battle raged. Eventually, the conservationists won. The line is now actively promoted, stations re-opened and used with a future as assured as any other in the country: which may not be saying too much.

Steam engines, privately owned, returned to work on the line in 1978. Now, most weekends, especially during the summer, steam specials run. There seems a bottomless market for this exercise in nostalgia. To see why, take up a line-side position and watch one of these highly polished behemoths fighting its way to the summit. It's so easy to be converted. Steam trains seem to blend into Dales scenery in a way that modern traction never does.

¤ Continue along Station road to the end. Here, turn left and immediately right down Chapel Street.

There are two fine buildings here. On the left, Ashfield House is now

The steps that carried a million feet on the back streets of Settle

reduced to the status of a social club. Nearly two hundred years ago, when it was built, a greenhouse grew vines and the superb garden was well tended. It was built for William Birkbeck, a local banker. His brother George founded Birkbeck College in London.

William Birkbeck's business partner was John Peart, a solicitor. He built Cragdale, opposite on the right. This now acts as the police station.

¤ Walk along Chapel Street to the end and turn right into Victoria Street. On the left, Delaney Court is new, but with buildings very much in keeping with the area; to a point. These are ordered, the rest of the area is delightfully higgledy-piggledy. The Court bungalows offer accommodation for older people. A fine grassed area with flowering cherry trees fronts this thoughtful development.

To the right can be seen the Masonic Hall and The Museum of North Craven Life. But the best is on the junction.

Tanner Hall was built in 1675 by Richard Preston. It was sold after his death in 1703 and soon became empty. During that time, it became known as The Folly, and it is known thus today. The stonework is absolutely superb, a fine and lasting tribute to the mason's art. It was finally restored in the 1970s and is occasionally open to visitors.

¤ Walk up the hill until the road almost doubles back on itself to the left at Junction Lodge. Take this, but also take care. It's very narrow and the locals seem to be unaware of speed limits.

On the right is the Zion Congregational Church, opened as an independent chapel in 1816. To the left a delightfully different Weavers Cottage carries the date 1841. Further along on the right, an old milestone is set into the wall.

¤ Past Weavers Cottage, look out for a flight of steps on the left. Take these – Well Steps – and keep right at the bottom, past the well, still fed by a spring and back up the slope. At the end of a length of spare ground behind a wall on the right, there is an archway. Turn right into here.

¤ Note: This is a very steep climb up Castleberg Crag. If you don't fancy this section, the Trail description will resume at *

¤ The unsurfaced but well-stoned path climbs steeply uphill in a series of switchbacks. Nearing the top, take the left-hand path to reach the summit.

OK, so it's been an effort to get up, but isn't it worth it. The only fleetingly disappointing thing is that a flagpole is discovered. This is set into a block of stone with initials and the date 1841, indicating that someone has actually been here before you. This was erected to mark the accession of Queen Victoria in 1837.

If the climb was breathtaking so is the view. Below, you can almost look down the chimney pots of the houses. To the left of the market square where this Trail started, the town hall roof is very attractive and the chimney stacks there delightfully different.

As your head lifts, the independent school at Giggleswick that has such a long list of famous alumni comes into view, followed by more hills reaching over towards Lancashire and the coast. And, there can be no finer vantage point in the area for photographing the steam trains and you can also keep an eye on your car to make sure it is not being tampered with.

¤ Walk along the ridge and down the far side. This is a very steep drop over boulders and it will be obvious why this was not recommended as a route up. Follow the switchback tracks back down to the road and turn right.

¤ *[Trail continues here, for those wishing to avoid Castleberg Crag]* Bear right at the next fork, but spare a glance for the left turn. Narrow and cobbled; Yorkshire personified. Continue to another junction. Here, with the Brewhouse on the corner, turn left, down towards the market square. Take the first left.

On the right halfway down the hill is another ancient building, this with a 1694 datestone. As the left turn is made, note the National Westminster Bank on the right. This was once a private residence owned by Dr. Charles Buck. He was a great friend of Sir Edward Elgar (1857-1934), the great composer and often played host to the man.

The curious building around the corner with the arched fronts is The Shambles. This was originally a seventeenth-century open market hall. Later, it was taken over by butchers and cattle were slaughtered there. Towards the end of the eighteenth century, the cottages above, together with the arches were added. Finally, in 1898, a second storey was added to the cottages.

¤   Walk to the end of the town hall, turn right into Cheapside, right around the building and back into the market square.

Note the fountain pillar, erected in 1863 to replace the market cross that had stood there for centuries.

Trail 11: Horton-in-Ribblesdale

Having reached Ribblesdale on the last Trail, it would not be polite to leave the area without popping up the valley a little further. Although Horton-in-Ribblesdale is minuscule, it's the place to where serious walkers head. The origin of this name means "Settlement on muddy land", and the village was in existence at the time of Domesday.

The Pennine Way – which we used on Trail 8 – and The Ribble Way come through here. The latter, opened on June 1st 1985, is a middle distance footpath following the route of the river Ribble from the estuary at Longton Marsh through Lancashire to its source, 70 miles (113km) away in the Pennines.

It came about as the result of a suggestion made by the Ramblers Association. The Countryside Commission and Lancashire County Council were involved initially, followed by North Yorkshire County

The squat tower of St Oswalds, Horton-in-Ribblesdale

Council and the Yorkshire Dales National Park who all joined forces to organise the route, waymarking and, occasionally, creating diversions where it was deemed necessary.

Other outdoor types congregate here. Cavers and potholers are well catered for and Pen-y-ghent towers to the east, all 2277ft (694m) of it. The mountain itself has been declared a Site of Special Scientific Interest in an effort to the preserve the rich flora and fauna up there. Nevertheless, there is a footpath right over the top of it: as I said, serious walker country.

Trail Facts

Distance:	1¼ miles
Clean Shoe Rating:	3
Map:	O.S. Landranger Series No 98
Start:	Roadside car park to north of village
Starting Grid Ref:	SD 808726
Car Parking:	As above
Refreshment:	A couple of pubs both serving food. For a real basic-but-solid meal, try the Pen-y-ghent cafe in the middle of the village.
Nearest TIC:	Cheapside, Settle, North Yorkshire , BD24 9ES – 01729 825192

¤ Leave the car park heading north, past the toilet block. This leads very shortly to a conglomeration of bridges, across the road from the New Inn. Cross the Ribble on a somewhat rickety footbridge and then return over the road bridges which cross that river and a beck.

¤ Having completed a very small but interesting loop, walk back down the road away from the bridges. This will take you past the information centre and cafe on the right, a newsagent/post office on the left, eventually arriving at the church. Turn left, into the gate, opposite The Golden Lion pub.

Walking down the road, glance to the right. There, a roadstone company are beavering away, trying to export the Yorkshire Dales en

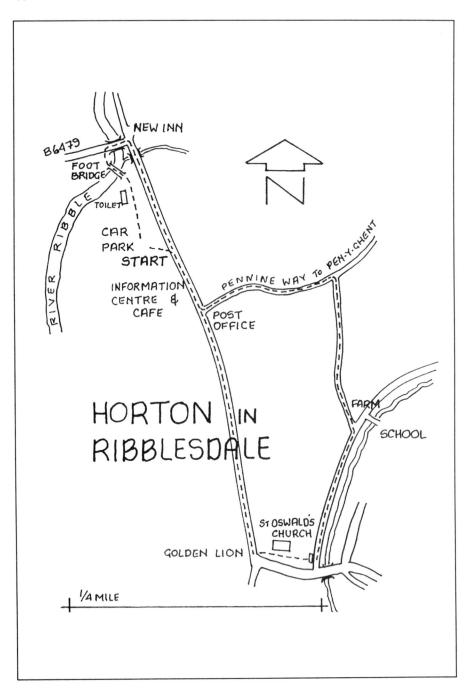

bloc. The hill is gradually being reduced to naught as layer after layer is removed.

Limestone quarrying is nothing new in this corner of the country. This particular area has only flourished since the arrival of the railway a century ago – see Trail 10. The availability of transport was the catalyst that saw these quarries develop.

Ever mindful of the type of visitor that reaches this area, the Golden Lion offer a good solid Yorkshire breakfast; doubtless welcomed by the outdoor lovers.

St Oswald's church is another with the typically Dales squat square tower. Much of the church is early twelfth century, although the tower and porch were built some three hundred years later. St Oswald lived from 605 to 642. He was involved in the construction of York Minster and was killed at Oswestry during a battle with the pagan king Penda.

The shallow pitched roof has a somewhat new appearance from the outside. This is not an illusion: it's new; and thereby hangs a tale of great spirit, tenacity and enterprise.

In 1989 the fabric of this place was in a mess. The roof leaked abominably, the heating boiler was shot and the organ wheezy. £68,000 was needed to sort the problems. With a possible congregation of only 450 people, none particularly wealthy, raising that sort of money was the stuff of dreams.

But no. A committee was formed. Local "names" were involved. These included "The Rochdale Cowboy", Mike Harding and playwright Alan Bennett. There were so many ideas forthcoming that it needed one committee member just to control them. Some were really different: a sponsored ascent of the Matterhorn for instance. Well, it beats the sponsored swim. So successful were they that the fund eventually topped £93,000.

There was an hiatus in 1990 when thieves stripped all the lead from the roof. They were spotted by a local man early one morning and apprehended later that day. As the chairman of the committee remarked, "They were caught lead handed." With the work finished in early 1996, the old place is fit for a few more years yet.

¤ Leave the church and turn left, through the low lych gate and turn left again. Note the huge stone slabs forming roofs over the lych-gates. More are used as paving stones in the churchyard.

Examine and admire the housing along this narrow lane. With a beck to one side, along with leafy trees, the ancient stone houses, well weather-beaten, look as though they have been part of the scenery since the creation. Again, many of these are quite low: everything is cowering from the weather. The only hint of modernity is provided by the fairly new school, just across the beck.

¤ Follow this track to where a bridge crosses the beck and a farm yard lies directly ahead. Here, turn left, away from the water and walk along this track to a "T" junction. Here, turn left again. This leads to the road. Turn right, back to the car park.

Trail 12: Clapham

The village stands in the shadow of Ingleborough 2372ft (723m), one of the Three Peaks of Yorkshire. It is the base for exploration of Ingleborough. Further up the path we use is the famous Gaping Gill pot and lots of energetic outdoor types start their expeditions into the bowels of the earth from here.

Trail Facts

Distance:	1 mile, plus Nature Trail (if used)
Clean Shoe Rating:	10
Map:	O.S. Landranger Series No 98
Start:	Dales National Park car park
Starting Grid Ref:	SD 745693
Car Parking:	as above
Refreshment:	Pubs, tea rooms and cafes, all around the start/finish area.
Nearest TIC	National Parks Centre, Clapham, North Yorkshire – 01524 251419.

¤ Leave the car park and turn left.

The National Parks Centre, by the car park has a choice display of geology, wildlife and natural history pertaining to these parts. There is also a small lecture theatre offering an eight minute video describing the area.

Along this road there is a selection of shops, cafes, tea shops, Ingleborough Cave Information Centre and even the cave rescue service.

¤ Walk to the main road and cross, following the road directly opposite which indicates that there is no through road. Continue down here, keeping Clapham Beck to your right.

A fine pub, The New Inn stands on the corner of this cross-roads.

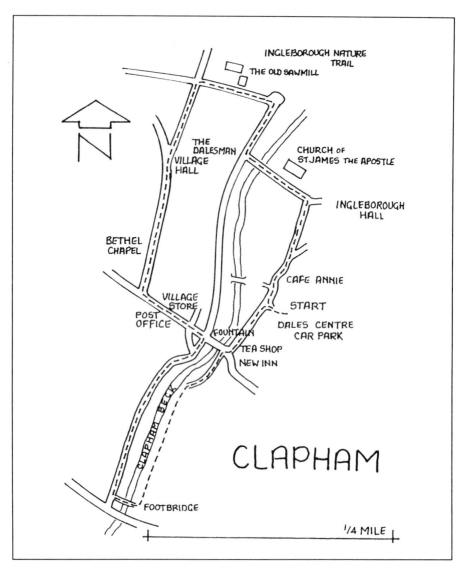

Serving food as well as drink, it's a good place to sample, perhaps after the Trail.

¤ As the path peters out, a small bridge crosses the beck. Take this and turn right, back up the other side of the water. On reaching the main road, turn left.

There is a drinking fountain located on the right-hand corner across the road, mounted in a quite attractive surround. The main shops in Clapham are located just around this corner. On the left, a post office and general stores, to the right, Clapham Village Stores, a newsagent plus.

¤   Walk along the road to and take the right-hand turn signposted towards the Village Hall. Walk along this road and, as it bears left, carry straight on.

The Bethel Chapel on the left was built in 1976. On the aforementioned junction, to the right is the Village Hall. Behind, the offices of The Dalesman Publishing Company.

The village was the original home of the "Dalesman" magazine. It first appeared in 1939 with the prefix "Yorkshire". The company now publish a wide range of books and magazines. Most are concerned with the various facets of life in this wonderful area, but have spread their wings to take in other regions of the north. This expansion has seen them move into offices near Skipton whilst still retaining the Clapham base.

¤   Carry on to the top and turn right on Eggshell Lane. The Old Sawmill is on the left. Here can be found the start of Ingleborough Estate Nature Trail. This is a 1¼ mile walk along a well kept path by the lakeside and then through the beautiful wooded grounds to the lower slopes of Ingleborough mountain and the imposing entrance to Ingleborough Show Cave. Admission to this walk is 30p (10p for children), but with a further fee payable if you want to see inside the cave.

The start is at Sawmill Cottage. Note the roof of a barn to the left of the cottage; the ridge has bowed delightfully with the passage of years. Inside this building, there is a waggon that was horse drawn and used for carrying felled trees around.

¤   After the old sawmill walk to the end of this road, turn right down Riverside and then take the first left, over the river. This leads past the church and, with an archway that is the entrance to Ingleborough Hall ahead, turn right with the road.

The church of St James the Apostle is very much larger than anything encountered thus far. The nave is wide and the roof is high, almost cavernous and with far less religious symbolism than in most other churches. It was rebuilt in 1814 with perpendicular tower and again in 1899 and 1903.

The Farrer family have much to do with the appearance of Clapham. They arrived in the village early in the eighteenth century and rebuilt Ingleborough Hall a hundred years later. This is now used as an outdoor education centre. Reginald Farrer (1881-1920) had a love of botany that saw him travel the world in search of rare plants. The descendants of many he brought back can still be seen in the area. The forest and lake are all the result of this family's labours.

That lake – on the forest walk – is entirely man made, constructed between 1810 and 1830, probably because it was fashionable at that time for the wealthy to have a boating lake.

¤   Follow this road down, past the main entrance to the hall, noting the delightfully misshapen footbridge over the river and turn left on reaching the car park.

The entrance to Ingleborough Estate Nature Trail and Cave

Trail 13: Ingleton

L ike Settle, visited on Trail 10, Ingleton was a small village on the Kendal to Keighley turnpike road of 1753. For all that, it was a sleepy little backwater until the railway age dawned. In 1849, a junction from the West Riding to Lancaster line at Clapham reached Ingleton and visitors soon found this pretty little town with the stunning scenery.

The name "Ingleton" means Beacon Town. Ingleborough at 2372ft (723m) is the mountain that dominates the view. That, like so many of the stirring features in this area are actually outside the limits of the town. But there is still much to see.

Trail Facts

Distance:	1 mile
Clean Shoe Rating:	10
Map:	O.S. Landranger Series No 98
Start:	Community Centre Car Park, Ingleton
Starting Grid Ref:	SD 695731
Car Parking:	See above
Refreshment:	All around the town
Nearest TIC	Community Centre Car Park, Ingleton North Yorkshire – 01524 241049

¤ Leave the car park heading east, away from the Tourist office and Community Centre. On reaching the road, turn left and walk up the hill, taking the first left down Main Street.

Note the red-topped French-style milestone on the corner. This gives the distance in miles (and kilometres) to Ingleton's twin town.

The doctor's surgery on the right started life as a Literary Institute in 1902.

¤ Walk through the shopping centre, past Ingleborough Nursing

Home and, as the road swings to the left, by Barclays Bank, turn right down a narrow little side road and walk straight ahead down Sammy Lane.

¤   Pass the Youth Hostel and bear left beyond it, following a narrow paved path. This leads down to a swimming pool and along the banks of the river Doe. Follow this to a bridge where the path leaves the river bank to join the road.

French-style milestone in Ingleton

One of the major attractions in this town is The Waterfalls Walk, 4¼ miles of scenic beauty. To access this from here, turn right, cross this river and the Twiss which runs almost alongside. Where the road turns left, the entrance to this walk will be discovered.

You will not, however, be the first. It was back in 1885 that this walk was arranged. How evocative are the names: Hollybush Spout, Pecca Glen, Snow Falls, Thornton Race; all conjure up visions of wild water and stark nature. Well, it's not quite so primeval, but the walk up the Twiss and back down the Doe is memorable. A warning though; this needs sensible footwear. An admission charge is made: £1.50 and 50p for children.

¤   Across the road, a gap in the wall gives access to a flight of steps. Note the coping stones on the wall; very old, the carving already severely weathered. Down the steps, and along, in front of the

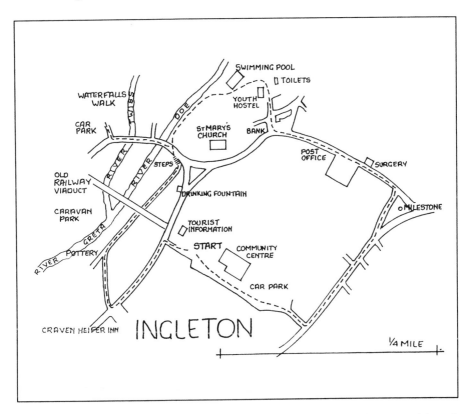

houses, under the massive old railway viaduct (now a Listed structure) and Ingleton Pottery on the right.

This is a retail outlet for the superb hand-made stoneware by Jill and Dick Unsworth. It takes only a few seconds looking through the window to appreciate the quality of what is on offer here. Visitors are welcome between 9.30am and 6pm daily.

¤   After the pottery, bear left, up the hill. Turn left at the top and walk towards the town.

The Craven Heifer is a seventeenth-century Thwaites house standing on the right. Good beer and a splendid menu make this a spot well worth a visit.

¤   A car park sign on the right returns the walk back to its start and the Tourist Information Centre, just inside the gate on the left.

As already noted, Ingleton is an ideal base for the wonderful natural attractions surrounding it.

The White Scar Caves are 1½ miles outside Ingleton on the Hawes road. Discovered as recently as 1923, they have been opened up for visitors and lit. All the usual glories associated with these phenomena are on offer: beautiful.

For the more adventurous, the sheer magnitude of Gaping Ghyll pot is available to mere mortals on Bank Holiday weekends. Waterproof and wellies are a must as you are lowered into the bowels of the earth on a bosun's chair. It's a hair-raising descent (and even more on the way back up) but the size and majesty of what is on offer makes the effort well worthwhile.

For those who can comprehend these things, it's 365ft

Down-to-earth food in Ingleton

(111m) deep, 450ft (137m) long and 130ft (40m) wide: you could fit a cathedral into the space. The TIC have information as each holiday approaches.

Trail 14: Dent

Dentdale, with the river Dee, is one of the smaller dales. It's also the only foray into Cumbria between these covers. And Cumbria it recognisably is, as the scenery becomes almost Lake District-like. Gone are the limestone crags, replaced by an altogether gentler milieu of hedges, fields and riverside meadows.

But, to confuse things even further, this was once in the west riding of Yorkshire. When those historic divisions were cast asunder by the Local Government Act of 1972, administration was transferred to Cumbria, itself a new entity taking in Westmorland and Cumberland. How long this situation will obtain is debatable as the latest thinking on boundaries is seeing some historic areas restored.

Moves are currently afoot to re-instate the Riding, a relic of the Danish Viking's time here. The original word was a "thirding" – which is why there were only three. Whether this area becomes Yorkshire again is doubtful, but ask any of the older residents where they live, and you will be treated to a diatribe about the foolishness of local government.

But, lift your eyes, and the hilltops make it unmistakably Dales country. The fells are still there and the starkness and grandeur that make this such an attraction to so many people are clear to be seen. To the north, Ayer Gill Pike rears up to some 1824ft (556m) whilst gentler slopes to the south lead to Crag Hill 2172ft (662m). Whernside, 2415ft (736m) is the next hill east. Dent station is on the Settle to Carlisle line and is the highest main line station in England (350m), but just happens to be five miles away to the east of Dent.

The narrow cobbled streets are still lined with the houses that doubled up as spinning and knitting works. This really was – quite literally – a cottage industry which survived until about a century ago. All the family used to engage in the several stages from shearing to transporting the finished product to be sold in Kendal market, a dozen or so miles away.

In those days, which actually lasted until the start of the twentieth century, first floor wooden galleries existed. Here was where the "Terrible Knitters e' Dent" toiled, needles clicking. Socks and gloves were prominent on the list of products, much being supplied for military use. With the mechanisation of knitting, production here faded and the population fell from over 1700 in 1801 to less than 600 now.

The difference of Dentdale is again emphasised here with colour-washed houses, rather than the forbidding plain stone to be found only a few miles east. Fortunately, this little village is not fully on the tourist map: yet. Its remoteness has saved it so far. This window on the past is quite superlative and almost demands a visit.

Trail Facts

Distance:	½ mile
Clean Shoe Rating:	10
Map:	O.S. Landranger Series No 98
Start:	Village Car Park, west of Dent on the Sedbergh road
Starting Grid Ref:	SD 704871
Car Parking:	As above
Refreshment:	Pubs in village
Nearest TIC	Community Centre Car Park, Ingleton North Yorkshire – 01524 241049

An attempt to walk around Dent now follows. It's such a small place and there are so many dead end alleys, each demanding some attention, that to appreciate this village to the full needs a degree of self-guiding. Follow the given route, but please don't be deterred from varying it, hopping off at odd angles, poking down narrow alleyways. Your curiosity will almost certainly be rewarded.

¤   Leave the car park and walk directly across the road, following a sign to The Shop on the Green. Bear left at the Green – the shop is on the right – and continue down this road. The Old Parsonage on the right was the birthplace of Adam Sedgewick.

He lived from 1785 to 1873, becoming one of our great geologists. The apogee of his career saw him in the chair of Woodwardian Professor of Geology at Cambridge. Despite travelling the world and becoming very famous, he never lost his love for Dent and the hills around, returning often during is life.

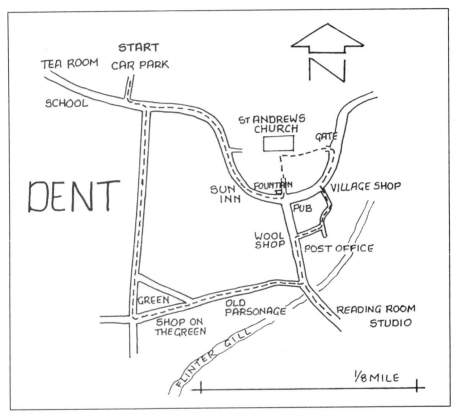

¤ This road then becomes very constricted and cobbled: almost unchanged for centuries. Turn right at the bottom, cross a pretty little bridge and turn left immediately after the Reading Room (1880). This is one of the alleys mentioned earlier. An artist's studio will be found amid the rest of the beauty.

¤ Turn around and walk back, past the post office and on reaching the wool shop on the left, turn right. Walk down this alley and keep to the left of an ancient house. This very narrow passage turns sharp left and gains the main road.

¤   Turn right, walk past the village shop to a gate which gives entry
    to the churchyard at its lowest point. Turn left towards the building.

The church in Dent is St Andrew's. It was built by the Normans
around 1080, but, as with so many other ancient ecclesiastical buildings, was rebuilt by the Victorians. There are still some Norman bits
remaining to be seen; pillars in the nave, and a blocked doorway.
There are Jacobean box pews here, carrying various dates, one being
1693.

Check out the chancel floor and admire the beautiful Dent marble.
There is also a fascinating curio from another age to be discovered in
here, and not a lot to do with the church either: a master's desk from
The Free Grammar School of King James, Dent. Complete with brass
plate under the lifting top, old inkwells with sliding lids are located
at each end.

¤   Leave the church and walk straight ahead to the road, turning right.
    A rough-hewn lump of Shap granite with a fountain on the corner
    here is the memorial to Alan Sedgewick.

Squat stone housing, so much a part of Dent

The George and Dragon, across the road to the left, is a free house selling Dent Brewery ales. Note the wall. A winged wheel with the letters CTC (Cyclists Touring Club) indicate how long this place has been popular with those hardy individuals. And, looking at the hills all around, hardy they most certainly were.

¤ Follow this road around until it returns to the car park.

The Sun Inn also sells Dent Ales. Their slogan, under a golden globe, complete with rays is: "Best Ale Under the Sun."

Further along, The Stone Close is a seventeenth-century tea shop (which also offers bed and breakfast) and The Dentdale Memorial Hall.

Trail 15: Hawes

Wensleydale: famous for cheese and beautiful Dales scenery. It is also the centre of tourism in this area. Compared to most towns and villages in this book, Hawes is a relative newcomer. The first real records of settlement are from the fourteenth century. The market, a vibrant centre of activity today, was not granted its Charter until 1700.

Unlike most other towns in the Dales, Hawes is towards the top of the valley, rather than nestling, sheltered, at the foot. This is probably explained by its late development; by the time things were starting to happen here, man had developed community living to a degree that life could still be tenable this far up the dale. It is now the highest market town in Yorkshire.

Sheep were the mainstay of the local economy. Even today, the livestock market is predominantly ovine. Pubs and hotels developed in the town to became coaching stations along the Richmond/Lancaster turnpike. The development of this road was the catalyst for Hawes. Until then, Askrigg – see Trail 17 – had been the centre of things. The road missed that town but not Hawes. The latter developed, Askrigg did not.

Yorkshire-style stile, for slim walkers only!

The railway from Northallerton and Leyburn arrived in 1876. This was soon followed by a branch from the Midland's Settle and Carlisle line. Suddenly, Hawes had good communications both east and west.

Much of the town's development and architecture reflect this boom. Quarrying, particularly, was well served by the iron road. The dairy industry developed on the back of rail-borne milk tankers. The smoothness and mellow flavour of Wensleydale cheese became known to a wider populace and visitors started to arrive.

Passenger services did not even last into the Beeching era: the last train left for Garsdale in March 1959, although freight towards Northallerton lasted for many years after.

Trail Facts

Distance:	1¼ or 2 miles
Clean Shoe Rating:	10. Extension Trail: 3
Map:	O.S. Landranger Series No 98
Start:	The Market Hall, Main Street
Starting Grid Ref:	SD 872898
Car Parking:	Alongside the Market Hall
Refreshment:	Hawes has everything
Nearest TIC	National Park Centre, Old Station, Station Road, Hawes North Yorkshire, DL8 3NT – 01969 667450

¤ With your back to the Market Hall, turn left and head out of the town.

The Market Hall was originally known as "Market House" and opened in 1902. The main hall is used for a variety of social events and the town's library is housed in one annexe. Across the road are just some of the inns and hotels that serviced the turnpike: Cockett's being the oldest. The inscription over the door reads: "Ano Dom 1668 God Being with who can be against".

The initials ATF refer to Thomas Forcett, who was a Quaker. The building was donated to them in 1754 as a rest house. Quakers gathered quite a strong following in the Yorkshire Dales. The founder

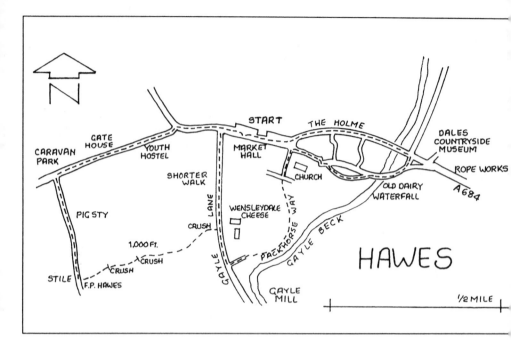

of The Religious Society of Friends, George Fox (1624 – 1691), brought his particular brand of Protestantism to the Dales in 1652.

Indeed, later that year at Sedbergh, just to the west of the Dales, the Quaker movement was put on a proper footing and formally established. Their Meeting House, now demolished, was on the corner of Brunt Acres Road, the burial ground across the road.

Fox gained many converts in this area and there are still meeting houses throughout the Dales. The Quakers did lose some of their support to Methodism in the next century as John Wesley visited the area.

¤   Continue up the road to the first junction on the left. Here, a decision has to be made. The shorter walk turns left up Gayle Lane and up the hill, the longer one continues along the main road and bears left at the next junction. Short Trailers pick up the narrative at *

On the corner of Gayle Lane, the local primary school. It's typically Victorian, completed in 1879. An old forge, still used by the local blacksmith, is on the right and a garage to the left. Here, over the years, both the town's hearse and early fire engine were housed. The house alongside, Steppe Haugh is now a licensed bed and breakfast. A stone lintel dates the building to 1643.

Just after the left, as the path climbs steeply, a huge stone slab is provided as a seat. A pause here gives the chance to appreciate Wensleydale at its finest. The Ure as a young river with sweeping scree-covered slopes beyond. Looking right, Hawes is almost at your feet with rolling hills all around. Most impressive.

¤   Walk up the road and take the first on the left, opposite a caravan park. Down this lane, a quite substantial agricultural building can be seen in a field to the left. This is no more that a pig sty, but note the quality of workmanship from an unknown mason centuries ago.

¤   Another 100 yards along (90m) on the left, a stone stile will be found giving access to the field: just. This is the route. Signposted "FP HAWES", it presents quite a challenge to surmount. Such a feat of mountaineering is needed to cross it that crampons and ropes would not be out of place.

¤   Directly across the field is another dry stone wall with a squeezer stile. Traversing this presents an altogether different problem. It is so narrow that, whilst bodies and legs are at right angles to the wall, feet are shuffling through the minuscule opening straight ahead – at right angles to your body.

¤   Another squeezer stile leads into the next field, with a gate at the far end. Here, atop Cross Rig, the path is 1,000ft (305m) high; more dramatic views.

¤   The next field is downhill and a clear track heads towards a gate into the road by a building. The official path leaves the field some yards higher through another squeezer stile. Turn right.

¤   This is Gayle Lane and a few yards along on the left is the Wensleydale Creamery.

Wensleydale cheese is made here: but not without a crisis or two over the years. The history of cheese making in Wensleydale disappears into the mists of time. It was recorded at Fors Abbey near Askrigg in 1156; turning milk into cheese or butter made for easier transportation and storage. It also meant that the product could be kept without going off, this being the days before refrigeration.

Factory production first started in 1897 and established Wensleydale cheese on the taste buds of an adoring nation. In 1966, it was bought by the Milk Marketing Board who continued production. Then, in 1992, the unthinkable.

Production finished and was transferred to – of all places – Lancashire. This caused great anger, both in the town and further afield. Epicureans fulminated whilst staff rebelled. With a great show of independence, a management buy-out was arranged and many jobs were saved.

Today, this delicately-flavoured cheese is rightfully popular throughout the world. It is possible to visit the creamery and watch its production. The Visitor Centre is open from 10am to 4.30pm daily, with most activity between 10am and 2pm. An admission charge is made.

Inevitably, there is a shop where you can buy the samples, and pretty well every shop in town also stocks it. There is also a museum and video and a first class tea room.

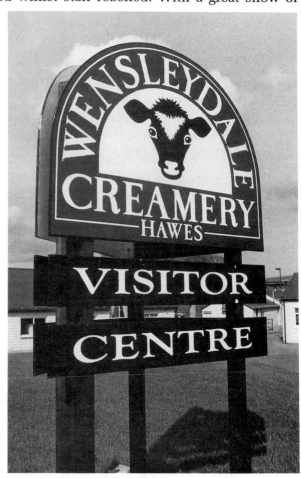

A welcoming sign to the centre for Wensleydale cheese production

The company have increased awareness of their product by enlisting the aid of those remarkable plasticine characters Wallace and Grommit into the sales drive.

¤   Continue along Gayle Lane for some 200 yards (180m) until the Trail meets the Pennine Way. Here, turn left along the old packhorse way down Bealer Bank.

On the right a multi-storied building is Gayle Mill, with Gayle Beck cascading past alongside. This water powered mill was built in 1784 as a cotton mill. Subsequently, it has been both a woollen mill and a sawmill.

¤   On reaching the church, pass to the left of the building, down through a courtyard to the road. Turn right and right again to visit the church.

The church is St Andrew's and is relatively modern. It was built during the mid nineteenth century, replacing the original which dated back to c1483.

A surprise in this conservative corner of the world is to see that the Roman Catholic church are welcomed into St Andrew's. They hold Mass on Saturday evenings, which fulfils Sunday obligations for the faithful; a rare example of co-operation between the two creeds.

¤   Continue down the right-hand side of the road and take the lesser lane that branches off to the right between Herriott's Hotel and Restaurant and Bee Lyne Knitwear shop. A few yards along on the left is Chapel Cottage, which is behind the chapel which fronts the main road. On reaching the river, cross the bridge, but pause a moment.

To the right is Gayle Beck and a beautiful waterfall. On the right of that, the Old Dairy is the original site of the Wensleydale Cheese factory. The opposite way is the Conservative Club on the left. This was once a corn mill. It also houses the premises of a wood turner who produces beautiful goods for sale.

¤   Continue down the road a little further, taking the main road sharp left, back along The Holme towards the town centre. Where that road meets the other near the church is Market Place. Walk along the main road back to the Market Hall.

There are endless buildings and fascination along this main street. Elijah Allen's for instance. From the outside, it has all the appearance of a good old fashioned grocer with good quality produce on sale. Surprisingly, the prices are not what you would expect from such an establishment and, whilst not competing with the Tescos of this world, offer an extensive range of items at reasonable cost.

At the Rock and Gem Shop on the left-hand side is a passage which curves gracefully round to the left to an antiquarian booksellers, Kit Calvert's. He was formerly a manager at the Wensleydale Creamery and also acquired a deep knowledge of Wensleydale, its people and dialect.

For a greater appreciation of Hawes and the Dales, visit the Dales Countryside Museum, on the site of the old station. In 1941, Marie Hartley and Emma Pontefract bought a number of old items at a sale in Leyburn. That purchase forms the basis of this museum. Joan Ingilby contributed much material over the next thirty years and also recorded the memories and stories of people who lived and worked in the Dales. The collection was eventually donated to the council and this museum, housed in old railway buildings, opened in March 1979.

Alongside, in the station yard is W.R. Outhwaite and Son. They are ropemakers and have a ropewalk that is fascinating and free. Further along, you can watch braided ropes being manufactured and have the chance to buy a variety of rope products.

A couple of miles from Hawes is Hardraw Force. This is the highest unbroken waterfall in England with a fall of over 98ft (30m) and well worth a visit, especially after a good rainfall.

Trail 16: Bainbridge

Bainbridge was once a the location of a Roman fort, VIROSIDVM sitting atop a low plateau called Brough Hill, overlooking the river Ure. This was established during the governorship of Julius Agricola around 80AD, at the time of the Roman's subjugation of the Brigante tribes.

During the time the Romans were here, it was rebuilt at least once. It is believed that marauding Brigantes sacked the place on periodic raids before the Romans subdued them.

Between 1146 and 1170 Conan, Earl of Richmond granted this area, which was part of a huge forested area, to Robert who built a village near Bain Bridge. These were to house twelve foresters and their families, and nine acres of land were also provided. By 1663, it had been sold to yeoman tenants. Today, it straddles the A684 as that highway ploughs along Wensleydale.

Stone roofs in Bainbridge

Being of such an antiquity, there are several fascinating legends attached to this area. Most intriguing is the one concerning a submerged city. Where Semerwater now lies, at the head of the Bain, there was reputed to be a large city. A traveller appeared seeking shelter. He was refused by all except an old couple on the edge of town. Next day, he caused a mighty flood to be visited on the place and all were drowned save the old couple.

For centuries, there was a tradition that at 9 o'clock every evening from September 28th until the following Shrove Tuesday, a horn was blown. This was to guide into the town anyone who may have become benighted on the moors. Sadly, as with so many of these traditions, a lack of local volunteers has seen the ages-old custom relegated to an occasional event.

Trail Facts

Distance:	1 mile
Clean Shoe Rating:	10
Map:	O.S. Landranger Series No 98
Start:	Bainbridge Post Office
Starting Grid Ref:	SD 934901
Car Parking:	Roadside in the area
Refreshment:	Only the pub
Nearest TIC	National Park Centre, Old Station, Station Road, Hawes North Yorkshire, DL8 3NT – 01969 667450

¤ Leave the post office walking south – alongside the right-hand side of that building.

The first building on the left was an old school. It offered:
"THE OLD DAME SCHOOL, MRS ELIZA BLADES, 186? - 1875 – READING WRITING ARITHMETIC 2d (1p) PER PUPIL PER WEEK."

¤ Walk to the limit of the house and then turn around and walk back, bearing left by the old chapel (1864) and up the hill.

The old building to the right, on the edge of the green is The Old

School. Currently disused, there are plans to convert it for use as studio/light industrial/retail/offices.

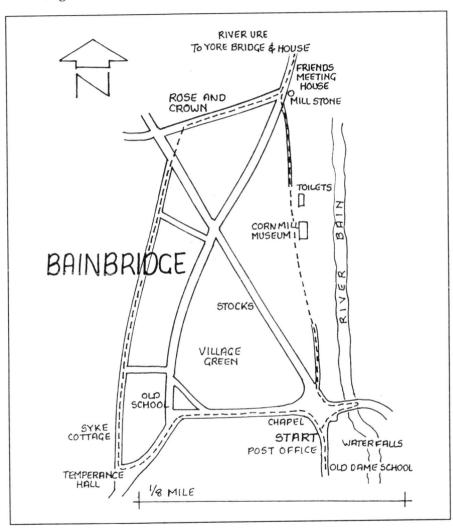

¤ Bear left here and at the end turn sharp right down a narrow lane past Syke Cottage (Bed and Breakfast). Just to the left at this turn you will find Bainbridge Temperance Hall. This is marked "Ano Dni 1910."

On the left is the Wesleyan Methodist Chapel dated 1836. Although well off for places of worship – there is still another one to come – there is no church of England building.

¤   Walk down this lane to the main road and cross, passing The Rose and Crown pub. This has a datestone inscribed 1443, but it carries the look of an early nineteenth-century rebuild.

¤   Walk down this road until the river Ure is reached.

On the right is a Friends Meeting House. For details of the Quakers in this area see Trail 15. Outside the building, a huge old millstone lies alongside the road, used now almost as a flower pot.

The bridge here, was designed by John Carr, who was also responsible for the magnificent Harewood House, near Leeds. It dates from the eighteenth century and was then known as the Yore Bridge.

¤   Turn round and walk back to the village centre. Just before the green there is a track to the left, Take this, which accesses the lower side of the green. Continue back to the post office.

There are toilets to the left along this section, followed by Low Mill, a restored corn water mill which has a permanent exhibition of furnished dolls houses and accessories for sale. Opening times are erratic. They are open every Wednesday from early July to mid September, 2pm to 5pm. Then, it is "Probably Open 2pm to 5pm Other Wednesdays and Holiday Weekends." A call to 01969 650416 to confirm. Other times by appointment. Admission is 75p for adults, 25p for kids.

Elsewhere on the green, a set of stocks can be seen.

Finally, before leaving, walk a few yards along the main road to the bridge. The Bain – at three miles in length – is reputedly the shortest watercourse in the country with the appellation "River". There are some very attractive falls to the right here.

Trail 17: Askrigg

Askrigg sits on the north side of Wensleydale, just across the river from Bainbridge. It was a prosperous settlement at Domesday and was the commercial centre of Wensleydale for centuries before Hawes gained the ascendancy. Before its decline, this was a quite wealthy village, home to a variety of small industries, the most unusual of which was clockmaking. Lead mining and textiles were the other mainstays.

Transport was the reason for the decline. When the turnpike came through the valley is was to the south side of the river: Askrigg was on the north. That was almost a death knell to the village. But a century later, when the railway was driven up the valley, it took the north side and Askrigg's renaissance began.

It managed to stay a pretty village much loved by visitors but the

The Kings Arms, Aysgarth – as featured on "All Creatures Great and Small"

essential simplicity of the place was unchanged. Then came the Alf Wight phenomenon. He was a vet who decided to augment his income with a book. "If Only They Could Talk", a series of delightful tales about his life and work in the area was published in 1970. To conceal his real name he adopted a nom de plume: James Herriot.

Although his practice was based in Thirsk, this was his "patch", a fact that the locals have cashed in on. The stories were set around his surgery in Darrowby. This fictional town had elements of Thirsk combined with several others.

When the BBC started filming these stories under the title "All Creatures Great and Small", the village selected to represent Dar-

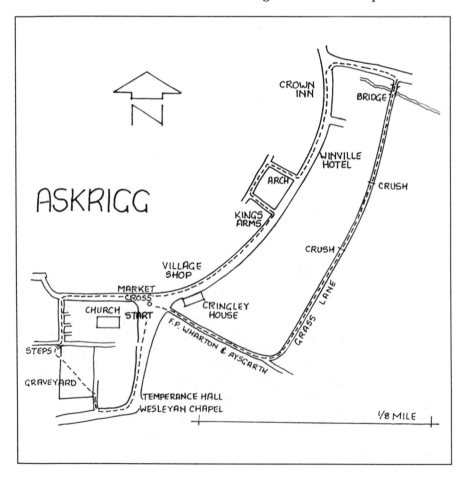

rowby was Askrigg. Just over the road from the market cross, Cringley House offered everything the location seekers wanted. During filming, this became Skeldale House, where James Herriot was supposed to live.

Much of the location filming was done at the small farms high in the remote Dales, and brought the area to a complete new audience. The effect did for Askrigg what "Last of the Summer Wine" has done for Holmfirth near Huddersfield. Although James Herriot died in 1996, his popularity – and that of the area he did so much to publicise – lives on.

The local council have produced an attractive small pamphlet called "The Herriot Trail". This details a scenic drive through Swaledale and Wensleydale, visiting many of the spots used in location filming, together with other sites that have connections with the story of this remarkable man.

Trail Facts

Distance:	½ mile
Clean Shoe Rating:	7
Map:	O.S. Landranger Series No 98
Start:	The Old Market Square
Starting Grid Ref:	SD 948910
Car Parking:	No car parks in the village, roadside as available
Refreshment:	Plenty in the village
Nearest TIC	National Park Centre, Old Station, Station Road, Hawes North Yorkshire, DL8 3NT – 01969 667450

¤ Stand by the village cross. Over the road to the left is the James Herriot house and a narrow alleyway runs off to the right of it. Walk down here. There is a sign – FP WHARTON and FP AYSGARTH – discreetly mounted on the wall of the building to the right.

This is instantly old Askrigg. The tiny cottages down here are clearly unchanged for centuries and full of character.

¤ Turn left with the path, up a slight rise, and through two squeezer stiles. This is now grass underfoot. This path takes you right around the rear of the village, unfolding marvellous views of the north side of Wharfedale as it does so.

¤   A little wooden bridge takes the path over a brook, then turn left. Swing left with the road.

The Crown Inn is on the right and several delightful stone houses, each with a cobbled forecourt are to be seen on the left. The Winville Hotel, a rather superior bed and breakfast has a quite ornate side entrance with two stone lions atop stone columns eternally on guard.

¤   Across the road is a pretty archway. Turn right through it and swing round to the left with the track. There are loads of old buildings in this courtyard, sadly, many derelict. Turn left again through the first archway, alongside the Kings Arms Hotel to the main road; turn right.

A chimney breast attached to the hotel looks in imminent danger of collapse. But it isn't. Leaning over at a crazy angle it actually presents a possible hazard to heads, so watch out and duck.

The Kings Arms has had its moment of fame in the past. It became Darrowby's Drovers Arms for the purposes of television. Unlike Skeldale House, it has returned to its original name as the TV series finished.

It also has a distinguished visitor book. One eminent name stayed there when painting in the area; J M W Turner. A further look at the man and his love of the Dales will be discovered on Trail 20.

¤   Keep to the right-hand pavement and pass the village shop. The window has the most delightful display of tins, stone bottles and stoppered bottles dating back half a century or more. Many old names, particularly from the confectionery world, are represented there.

¤   Stay on the right, past the start of this Trail and continue along the road, church on the left. On reaching the Old School House, turn left and walk to the fence at the bottom.

There are numerous tiny courtyards on the right. Each is crammed with houses, all peaceful and away from the visitors to Askrigg who seldom find these more interesting corners.

The last row carries a plaque defining them as "New Houses". The date follows: 1834! The best view of these probably comes after you have entered the graveyard.

¤   By the fence turn half right, down a short flight of steps rather than full right through a squeezer stile. At the bottom of the steps, turn left beside the wall and a few paces along turn left into the graveyard. Follow the track, diagonally right, to an exit in the far right-hand corner. Down a lane, this leads to the road; turn left. Walk up this road, around the corner to the entrance to the church yard.

There is an old Wesleyan chapel on the right-hand side, dating from 1878 and the Temperance Hall next door dated 1906, now the village hall. There are also toilets here. The Apothecary's House is a three storey building on the right. Next door carries a 1687 datestone.

St Oswald's, Askrigg is quite different from other churches encountered so far. There is a ring of six bells which were renovated as recently as 1992 and first rung on Easter Day. The building itself dates from 1446 and was rebuilt in Late Perpendicular style on the site of a previous church. There was further rebuilding in 1770 which produced a large expansive church, far removed from the tiny low towered ones.

There are a number of large houses around Askrigg, all still in private hands. The Metcalfe family have been landowners in this valley for centuries. One, Thomas, accompanied Henry V to Agincourt as leader of the Wensleydale Archers.

One of their houses, Nappa – a mile to the east of Askrigg – was where Lady Anne Clifford stayed during her journeys around the area. It's also said that she once entertained Mary Queen of Scots there when she was held at Bolton Castle in 1568/9.

Trail 18: Keld

Into Swaledale for the first time in this book. And what better place to start than almost at the head of the Dale. Only a short Trail this, but for surroundings of sheer beauty, it is probably unsurpassed between these covers; which is saying something. Keld itself is – frankly – nothing startling, but it is totally unspoilt by even the slightest hint of modernisation. Indeed, it almost comes as a shock to find a telephone box at the head of the village: as though such facets of modern living ought not to have penetrated this far.

The name "Keld" is – again – Old Norse, meaning "spring or well". Its original label of "Appletreekeld" has been abbreviated over the centuries to something a little more manageable.

The river Swale, Norse for "swift", rises a little to the west of Keld and careers down a series of waterfalls and rapids, along a limestone bed before becoming more staid and flowing generally east for some sixty miles to join the Ure near Aldborough.

It's a land of stark beauty. The Pennine Way crosses Swaledale here, Waterfalls are the main attraction, but with somewhere like Crackpot Hall in the vicinity, it's got to be worth visiting.

Sadly, this is no more than a ruined farmhouse now. And the name? Well, anything less connected with insanity would be hard to find. Again, the old Norse language gave us "a hole where are to be found carrion crow".

Sun dial, Keld Congregational Chapel

Trail Facts

Distance:	½ mile
Clean Shoe Rating:	2
Map:	O.S. Landranger Series No 92
Start:	Keld Village Car Park
Starting Grid Ref:	NY 893013
Car Parking:	As above. This is almost by the river in a farmyard. The farmer has let his field for the park. It's unpaved and costs between 50p and £1.
Refreshment:	None
Nearest TIC	National Park Centre, Old Station, Station Road, Hawes North Yorkshire, DL8 3NT – 01969 667450.

¤ In the left-hand corner of the car park, diagonally opposite the entrance, is a track. This leads down to the river and a simply superb waterfall. This is part of a camping field, and there is a rudimentary path from the water's edge to the right taking in the whole of this dramatic scene.

¤ Retrace your steps back to the car park and back to the lane. Walk up the way you came, pausing to notice a tiny little cottage to the right, huddled against two large buildings. There is also the Congregational chapel. This was founded in 1791 and enlarged in 1818. There is a delightful sun dial which gives the exact latitude and longitude of Keld.

¤ Walk up the hill and, at a "Y" junction, take the right-hand fork. This soon leads up to the "main" road. Here, turn left, walk along past the Youth Hostel and a couple of other buildings to the next road junction

¤ Turn left again and walk down the hill into the housing and back to the car park. Not much of a walk, and not a lot to see in the way of sterling architecture. But, with Kisdon, east of the village, some 1637ft (499m) high and the river, there is enough beauty and drama to satisfy even the most jaded palate.

There is no church here. This created a problem for burial centuries ago. The nearest consecrated ground was in Grinton. A track around

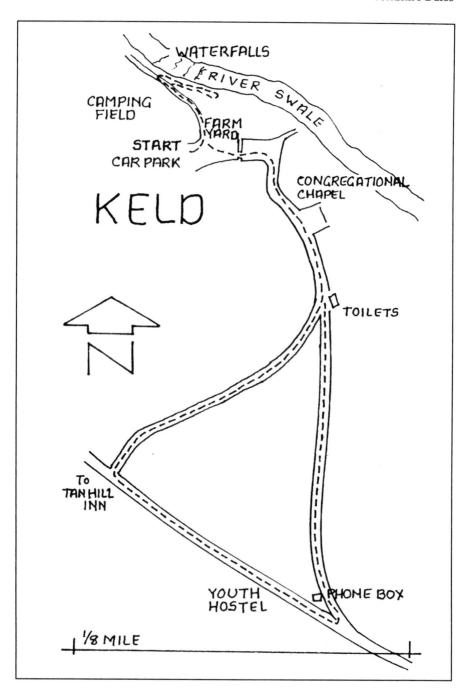

WATERFALLS

RIVER SWALE

CAMPING FIELD

FARM YARD

START CAR PARK

CONGREGATIONAL CHAPEL

KELD

N

TOILETS

To TAN HILL INN

YOUTH HOSTEL

PHONE BOX

⅛ MILE

the north face of Kisdon, above the river, was once known as "The Coffin Road". It was along here that the dead were borne on their way to burial. After consecrated ground became available at Muker (see Trail 19) in 1580, the journey was considerably reduced.

Despite its appearance, Keld was once a place of some activity. Lead mining was carried on in the hills all around and the population was considerably more than it is today.

There was even coal to be won at Tan Hill, four miles (6.4km) north of Keld. This was used to smelt the lead ore. There was once a pub in the village called the Cat Hole Inn; now long gone. But the Tan Hill Inn still survives. It's worth a visit if only because it's the highest licensed premises – some 1732ft (528m) – in England.

Now, as will be evidenced all around, the only industry in Swaledale is sheep rearing. Indeed, the eponymous breed, a hardy beast, is everywhere around.

Trail 19: Muker

Yet again, the name of Muker has Norse origins, translating to meadow. And what meadows. Lush green fields, a gaunt stone barn seemingly in every one, marks this area as very different from Keld, only a few miles further up Swaledale.

Muker is actually build back from the valley of the Swale, on a slope that faces Straw Beck, just before it empties into the Swale. It was built up here for good reason. Floods have caused severe damage over the centuries. In 1899, a particularly turbulent one almost washed the entire place away.

Trail Facts

Distance:	½ mile
Clean Shoe Rating:	10
Map:	O.S. Landranger Series No 98
Start:	The Car Park, alongside Straw Beck
Starting Grid Ref:	SD 910978
Car Parking:	See above
Refreshment:	One pub and a tea room
Nearest TIC	National Park Centre, Old Station, Station Road, Hawes North Yorkshire, DL8 3NT – 01969 667450.

¤ Return to the road and turn left, across the river. Walk along this road until a lesser road moves off to the right, uphill. As this turns sharp left, there is a delightfully small reading room on the junction. A little higher on the same side is the church.

This was built in 1580 and restored in 1890 with much of the interior altered. One particularly unusual – and welcome – feature of the church records are a series of photographs. They record the incumbents from 1921 to the present time There are also two photographs taken just before the alterations were undertaken in 1890 The clock

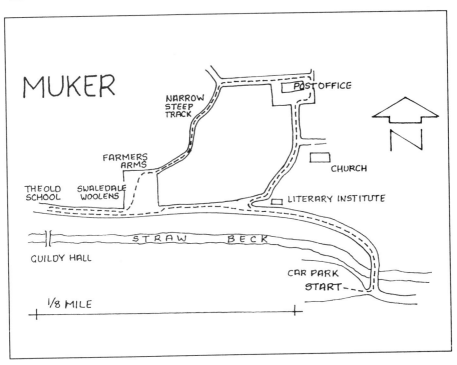

in the tower was installed on June 22nd 1911 to mark the Coronation of King George V.

¤   At the top of the hill is a small shop and village post office. Turn right and first left, to come back alongside the rear of the post office. Carry on along this ever narrowing lane, past the delightful stone housing until the paved surface ends.

¤   Down a steep track, through an "S" bend and the path arrives at the courtyard to The Farmers Arms.

Swaledale Woollens – to the right – was opened in 1974 with the intention of making available the traditional Dales crafts of hand knitting and crochet work. Using the wool from Swaledale sheep, a large group of home knitters produce the range of articles available for sale in this cottage shop.

Inside the building, in addition to the items for sale, there are some fascinating pictures and information about the sheep and the history of knitting in Swaledale.

To the left is a tea room/restaurant with the village shop next door.

Muker Literary Institute

The Farmers Arms is a free house dating from 1827. The main brew on offer is Theakston's that Masham brew of almost mythical quality. Food too is first class. A good and varied menu is served daily and portions will match any appetite nurtured on Dales air and exercise.

A few yards to the right is the old school. This was the only place that afforded an education to Richard Kearton (1862-1928). He and his brother Cherry (1871-1940) were both born in Thwaite, a mile to the west, and were to become pioneers in wildlife photography and accomplished naturalists. Plaques marking their time at the village school can be seen in that building.

¤ From the school, cross the road and turn left. Guildy Hall, complete with a bridge over the brook, is private, but looks a very des. res. Walk back along the road to the car park.

Trail 20: Reeth

R eeth is a small village to the north of the river Swale, with its own attractive Arkle Beck which empties into the main river close by. It's another delightful Swaledale village, built on the side of a hill.

Its position, where Swaledale and Arkengarthdale meet saw Reeth assume an important place in history. A market Charter was granted in 1695, producing further growth. This was compounded in 1741 when the road up Arkengarthdale towards Westmoreland was turn-piked. By then, the hills were alive to the sound of ... lead mining!

Here, as in a dozen other Dales villages, this was the only other major employer after agriculture. And, bearing in mind that it was always a struggle to make this poor quality land yield any substantial rewards from those labours, it certainly played its part in the histori-cal scheme of things.

Swaledale Folk Museum in Reeth

Hand knitting was also a busy local cottage industry and the market soon expanded to no less than seven fairs in addition to the regular Friday markets.

But those boom days are now gone for ever. Today, the main trade is extracting money from visitors. This is done in the most delightful way and the multitude of craft shops and other retail outlets offer very good value for money.

Not that they lie back lazily: far from it. Pride in their gorgeous village is such that entry into "Best Kept Village in North Yorkshire" is now a regular occurrence. And they win. The latest recorded success was in 1995. Bearing in mind that most of the villages we have visited throughout this book are eligible, there is clearly the potential for still more success.

Trail Facts

Distance:	1 mile
Clean Shoe Rating:	3
Map:	O.S. Landranger Series No 98
Start:	The Kings Arms, The Village Green, Reeth
Starting Grid Ref:	SE 038993
Car Parking:	All around the Square
Refreshment:	Ditto
Nearest TIC	Thornborough Hall, Leyburn, North Yorkshire DL8 5AB – 01969 620369

¤ With your back to the pub door, turn left, uphill and walk to the top of the square. Opposite a set of toilets is The Buck. Turn left here and follow the road along, past the delightful old-fashioned bakery.

This serves very tasty wares. The bread is high quality and they also keep a good line in pies and pasties. Open every day from 9.30am to 4pm except Sunday when you can visit between 10am and 4pm.

¤ Turn left, just a short distance along, past the fire station. This leads alongside some very ordinary council-type houses.

A few yards beyond this turn on the same side as the baker's is a "crafty" retail area. Here Stef Ottevanger designs and creates models

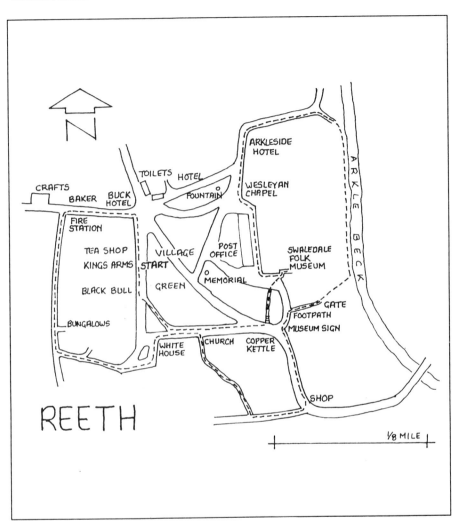

REETH

and wall plaques. Her theme is The Dales and the animals therein: Swaledale sheep feature very strongly. These creations are exquisite and well worth a look. Open Easter to October from 9.15am to 4pm, Monday to Friday and 10.30am to 4pm Sundays. Stef's number is 01748 884498.

Next door, Philip Bastow creates fine hand-crafted wooden furniture using essentially English wood. Again, quality workmanship is available from 9am to 5pm Monday to Friday, 9am to 4pm Saturdays, 01748 884555.

On the left is a cul-de-sac with bungalows. Immediately after, on the left some fifty yards before a main road junction, a narrow lane runs off for some thirty yards before developing into an alleyway.

¤ This passes some delightfully quaint housing before reaching The White House, slightly left of straight ahead. This is actually a tea room and is located at the bottom of the square. Pass to the left of this building and turn right along its frontage.

¤ Take the first right which is a little alleyway. This turns left, along the frontage of houses to another alley. Turn right, walk to the end and turn left. This drops towards the lowest part of the village, joining the road coming in from Richmond.

¤ Turn left, to the end and left again by the shop. Walk back towards the village centre, bearing right, following a sign to Swaledale Folk Museum. After only a few yards, another track leaves to the right with a footpath sign. This narrows considerably before plunging down towards Arkle Beck.

During the summer, this section can become quite overgrown with brambles and nettles; unprotected legs beware.

¤ On reaching the beck, pass through the gate and turn left along the path. This accompanies the water for a short time before moving away left and forming a small road. At this point, there is a quite splendid view up Arkengarthdale.

¤ Bear left with this road, up the hill, past the Arkleside Hotel. A lovely cobbled courtyard is passed along this section. The Wesleyan chapel is next to be encountered and then, keep left at this corner, though a little dog-leg and on the left is an cobbled alleyway leading to Swaledale Folk Museum.

On the corner, opposite the chapel is a water fountain. This was the first clean water supply to the town. The tanks were erected "...by the munificence of Geo. Robinson Esqre of Richmond 1868."

The museum is an excellent spot to fill in the background to much that has been touched upon between these covers. The history of lead mining is examined, together with the processes involved between digging out and coating the church roof.

Farming – of course – gets the treatment, together with the mock-up of a Swaledale housewife's kitchen, complete with what was needed to make butter, wash the family clothes and feed them. It also examines the surprisingly high incidence of non-conformist religion and why the population fell so dramatically when the industrial revolution got under way. Not huge, it's still a worthwhile place to spend some time. Opening hours are: 10.30am to 5pm from Good Friday to October 31st, and the Curator, Mrs D Law can be contacted on 01748 884373.

¤ Leave the museum and walk along the cobbled street and turn left on reaching the village green. This leads down a narrow pathway to the road. Cross the road to The Copper Kettle and follow the perimeter back to the Kings Arms.

This will take you past The Garden House pottery and the Congregational church. Needless to say, there is a James Herriot connection here. Langhorn House, opposite The Buck Hotel was the first Skeldale House in the original film and the bar of The Black Bull was taken over to film interiors at that time.

Joseph Mallord William Turner (1775-1851) is arguably Britain's finest landscape artist. Although a Londoner, he developed a love affair with the Dales as young man.

He first visited Yorkshire in 1797 and made three further visits in his life. The final one was during his last great artistic period. This started in 1829 when he again visited Italy. Two years later he was back in his beloved Dales.

Still to come from that master brush was The Fighting Téméraire (1839) and Rain, Steam and Speed (1844). His depiction of a rainstorm could well have been drawn from his Dales experiences.

Today, there is a The Turner Trail leaflet. This maps out Swaledale and Wensleydale, picking out some of the spots where Turner worked. Seats are provided, making it possible to look out over views hardly changed since the master captured them for posterity.

Trail 21: Leyburn

Very much in the lower reaches of Wensleydale, Leyburn is surrounded by grass, rather than hill and mountain as is the lot of most other villages and towns in this area.

Sadly, it's a town that has lost much of its character: a place that used to have many points of interest. They have now generally disappeared under redevelopment that took place before the historical value of such things was recognised.

There is a settlement called Leborne mentioned in Domesday, but it was never more than a hamlet. It was the effects of the plague that struck Wensley in 1563 – see Trail 23 – that saw Leyburn's star in the ascendancy.

A site for the market was needed as Wensley became a

A hidden corner of Leyburn

ghost town and it was to Leyburn that the honour fell. Development followed and by 1686 there was so much demand that a new Charter was granted increasing its frequency from fortnightly to weekly.

Trail Facts

Distance:	1¼ miles
Clean Shoe Rating:	4
Map:	O.S. Landranger Series No 99
Start:	Market Place, Leyburn
Starting Grid Ref:	SE 112905
Car Parking:	On street around the centre
Refreshment:	All around the centre
Nearest TIC	Thornborough Hall, Leyburn, North Yorkshire DL8 5AB – 01969 620369

¤ Leave the Market Place heading north towards Grove Square which is to the right of the Bolton Arms. Once in the square, there is much to see.

Leyburn Hall is a private house that has recently been converted to provide bed and breakfast accommodation. It's also Grade II Listed. The building is well over two hundred years old. Grove Square itself was the original site of Leyburn Market. There is also a delightful alley to the right-hand side leading to Chandler Gallery that is old Leyburn personified.

¤ Walk up the lane opposite – Shawl Terrace – signposted towards The Shawl. At the top, turn left and then right a few paces further along, through a kissing gate into a field. Walk up here until the edge of a playing field is reached. In the wall is a squeezer stile. Pass though it and turn right.

The Shawl is a superb vantage point with views to the west up Wensleydale. This unusual name comes from the Anglo-Saxon word for splintered rock: Schale. A somewhat mundane truth but well obscured by a local legend.

During her time at Bolton Castle, Mary Queen of Scots escaped her captors. This ridge was part of a packhorse road that came from the

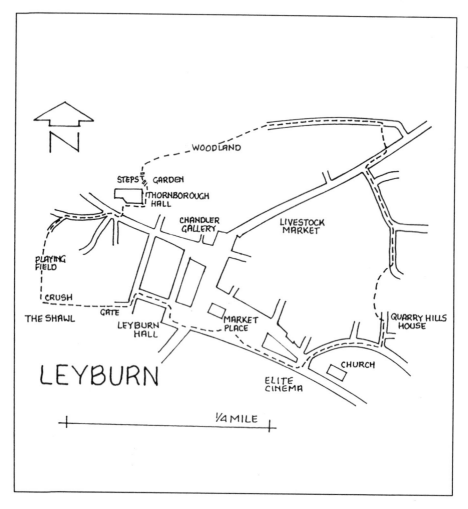

castle, and Mary used this road, dropping her shawl hereabouts as she fled.

Whether she escaped or no, it did not allow her to avoid a savage end to her life at Fotheringhay Castle in Leicestershire. And with a story like that, full of mystery, intrigue and dash, who needs to know about splintering limestone?

¤   Walk alongside the soccer field and at the end, walk down a narrow lane. On reaching the semi-paved road, bear half right and walk to the bottom. Cross, and a few yards to the right is an entrance into the grounds of Thornborough Hall. Take this, turn right and then left around the low side of the building.

Thornborough Hall was once a fine Georgian mansion built for the eponymous family. In due course it was bought by Joseph Hansom, who gave his name to the cab which he patented in 1834. It became council owned in 1966 and how houses administration offices, the tourist office and library.

And, should the exterior look vaguely familiar, it probably is. It was used during filming of "All Creatures Great and Small" as the Ministry of Agriculture building. See Trails 17 and 25 for more information on this popular series.

¤ Directly ahead is an extensive garden and lawn with a huge brick wall beyond. This was once the Hall's garden. At the left-hand end of this wall are three steps. Climb these and turn right up more, noting the fine rose garden to the right, on top of – and behind – the wall.

¤ Climb the hill, through a pleasantly wooded area. At the top, a road starts off downhill past some 1960s style bungalows. Almost at the bottom, where the housing gets markedly older, a narrow alley to the right gives access to the main road. Should you miss this, on reaching the main road, turn right and arrive at the same point.

¤ Cross the road and walk down Woodside, past housing not normally associated with these Trails. But, "no pain- no gain": there are still some treasures to behold.

¤ Bear right with Woodside and, after walking alongside some iron fencing, a wide track on the right leads to some garages. Continue past these to Quarry Hills House. This was built in 1877 as the parish workhouse and is a listed building. At the bottom, turn right and follow the road round towards the main road. Here, turn left to visit the church.

Amazingly, Leyburn was without a parish church until 1883. The building is pleasant without holding much that compels attention. Turn right on leaving the church and walk back into the Market Square.

Across the road The Church Room is where, amongst others, the local

Women's Institute meet. The Elite Cinema, a few yards away, is a fascinating building that contains seats with the most leg room this writer has ever encountered in such a place. It's built on a level and has a stage. Having lost its status as a cinema when that medium went into free-fall decline, it was used mainly for theatrical presentations under the name of "The Playhouse". Now restored to its former function, there are still "live" shows here from time to time. Its a wonderful asset to such a small community and appears to be well supported.

On the right, The Sandpiper Inn, another venerable building. The rest of the Square is a delightful amalgam of old and new. Particularly note the old Town Hall in the centre. Now used for retail purposes, it once held fire station, magistrates court and gaol.

Trail 22: West Burton

West Burton is something of an anachronism. Look at the place, set on the south side of Bishopdale and it's as pretty a village as you could wish to see. Now analyse that opinion. What is there that makes it stand out? Where are the magnificent buildings, abbey ruins, castle, church? And the answer is: nothing and nowhere. Yet, it is that very same plain-ness that appeals. In fact, it also attracts the powers-that-be, because the whole village is a Conservation Area.

There is a historical record of the village before the Normans took over the area, but it never grew as did other settlements nearby. In later centuries, much of West Burton was occupied by quarry and mine workers. Walden Beck runs through the village but the main roads dodges it. Most of the housing gathers around a large rectangular green. Let's look at this understated attraction.

A basic shelter at the edge of West Burton village green

Trail Facts

Distance:	1¼ miles
Clean Shoe Rating:	6
Map:	O.S. Landranger Series No 98
Start:	Village Square
Starting Grid Ref:	SE 016866
Car Parking:	All around the village
Refreshment:	Pub only
Nearest TIC	Thornborough Hall, Leyburn, North Yorkshire DL8 5AB – 01969 620369

The stepped octagonal obelisk marks the centre of West Burton and the place from which we will start. The exact purpose of this object, built in 1810 is unclear. It is certainly not a memorial and West Burton has never had a market. The nearest church is at Aysgarth – of which more later – so any religious significance is doubtful. Whatever, it adds to the overall view.

Again, as in Trail 7, the village is so small that we can adopt the figure-of-eight method of exploring everything worth a look.

¤   Head straight up the hill, away from the village, with the upper green on the right. A school stands behind this. At the brow of a hill, the road runs into a farm yard. Take the left path, between a barn and low cottage. This becomes a narrow track signposted "FP DAME LANE – 200 YDS". Follow this to the lane at the end and turn left.

Walking along this track, take note of all those delightful views to the left. It is possible to look over the top of West Burton and over to the north slopes of Wensleydale. The ruined shape of Castle Bolton stands out clearly. This is examined in detail during Trail 23. Exquisite.

¤   This returns the Trail to West Burton Square. Walk diagonally across towards the pub and along this street.

The last building before reaching the square is a very pretty Methodist chapel. Also from this point, it is unusual to look across to the village

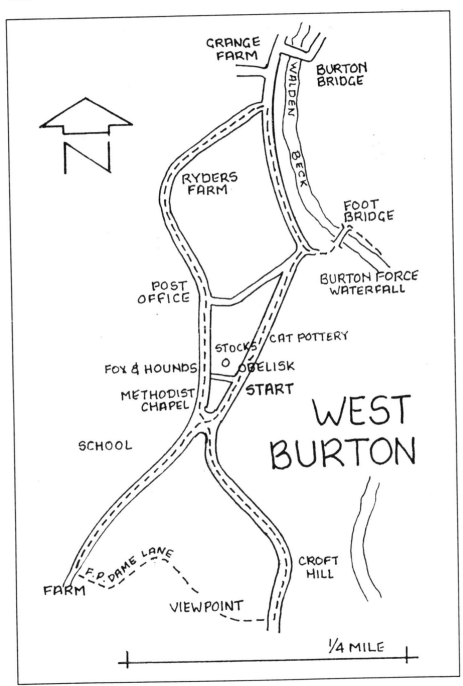

houses and note that, whereas thus far, virtually every roof of any age at all had been stone slabbed, several here are slated.

The Fox and Hounds is a free house selling Black Sheep ale amongst others. Beyond, the post office. On the right is a ramshackle old building the gable end of which provides the shelter for a village seat.

¤ Follow the road right down to the bottom, then, almost by the river, turn right.

All the way down this street are ancient buildings, friendly but never dramatic. One that particularly attracts is Ryders Farm on the right; very ancient.

¤ The road soon turns right to regain the centre of West Burton, but the walk detours to reach probably the most dramatic part of this Trail.

¤ Continue straight ahead and after only a very short distance, Burton Force is encountered. This is a truly beautiful waterfall and can be approached from either bank. Walk up, stand and admire. And, if it has been raining recently, the effect is that much more dramatic. On the far side is a seat, one of those provided as part of the Turner Trail.

¤ Return from the waterfall and turn left, up the hill back towards the square. On the right is a very ornate house – The Mount – whilst across the road, a castellated roof-line augments the already pretty scene. The datestone 1656 on this house gives an indication of its antiquity. Then The Cat pottery is just that; a small owner-run pot works specialising in feline shapes. If you are a cat lover, you will be entranced by the place.

There is also a set of stocks almost at the end of this Trail. Judging by the numbers of these instruments we have encountered in the various places we have visited, the White Rose County must have been very keen on their use: or perhaps they just preserve things better up here.

Close By

The village of Aysgarth is a little distance away, but between there and West Burton is Aysgarth Force, just north of the main A684 Leyburn to Hawes road. Here, the river Ure is crossed by a handsome stone bridge.

This was built in 1534 for pack horses. In 1788, due to increasing traffic demands (where have we heard that before) its width was doubled: one half is two hundred years older than the other. From underneath, which side is which is clearly visible.

Aysgarth Force is a magnet. Stretching over a mile in total, there is a car park and footpath which allows full exploration of the various falls and rapids. J M W Turner was also mightily impressed. He painted the Lower Fall, furthest from the car park, but most impressive.

Close by, the church of St Andrew contains some of the finery that was housed in Jervaulx Abbey until the Dissolution. The ornately carved wood in the screen to the south side of the chancel came from there, as did the vicar's chair.

At one time, St Andrew's was parish church for the whole area, offering pastoral services to the inhabitants of some 80,000 acres (32,375ha).

The Yorkshire Coach and Carriage Museum is housed in what was an old mill, hard by the bridge, originally built in 1784 to grind corn. This was destroyed by fire in 1853 but rebuilt and has since had a variety of other uses over the years, including the milling of flour from 1912 to 1959. Declared redundant by its owners, it was then put to its current use in 1967.

This diverse collection of horse-drawn carriages and vehicles is housed on three floors. There are over fifty exhibits and thirty scale models. It includes such treasures as a char-à-banc, a manual fire engine, a Hovis bread van and a Hansom cab.

In addition, there is the Yore Mill Craft Shop and Mill Race Tea Room: you can buy craftily and drink racily after enjoying the museum.

Trail 23: Wensley

Wensley had the first market in the Dales, receiving its Charter in 1202. Others followed and the place lost much of its significance. In 1563 the black death visited. The few survivors fled, leaving a ghost town. The market was moved to Leyburn and Wensley festered, uninhabited and unloved for almost a century. Then, in 1678, Bolton Hall was built and many of the estate workers moved back into Wensley. The Hall was destroyed by fire in 1902, but rebuilt. The remains of the original house can be seen.

Today, this pretty village, spoilt only by the busy A684 steaming through the middle, offers only a very short Trail but crams enough interest in those few hundred yards to match places twice its size.

What will soon become apparent is that this is very different from other walks in this area. Gone are the craggy hills and steep-sided valleys, replaced by arable fields and trees.

The waterfall on Wensley Brook

Trail Facts

Distance:	½ mile
Clean Shoe Rating:	10
Map:	O.S. Landranger Series No 99
Start:	Outside the church, Wensley
Starting Grid Ref:	SE 092895
Car Parking:	On side roads
Refreshment:	One pub only
Nearest TIC	Thornborough Hall, Leyburn, North Yorkshire DL8 5AB – 01969 620369

The parish Church of the Holy Trinity dates back to 1245, built on the site of an earlier, Saxon, church. A further rebuilding in 1719 provides what is to be seen today. Inside it's a delight. The choir stalls are particularly worth inspection. They were made in 1527. John Wesley was one name who preached here, this in 1743. There are also several items salvaged from Easby Abbey at the Dissolution. It was also used as the location for James Herriot's filmed wedding in the TV series "All Creatures Great and Small".

¤ Leaving the churchyard turn right, away from the main road. This passes a row ancient estate houses, connected with the Hall.

¤ Down the dip, cross the bridge and take the first road on the left. This leads uphill, passing some more delightful housing.

¤ As the road bears right, past a house on the left called Beckside, a track continues ahead. This is the Trail. It's a green lane, covered with wild garlic, the scent of which is all-pervasive. The way ahead is also quite steeply uphill.

¤ At the top, on meeting the road, turn left. A few yards along is a bridge over Wensley Brook. Turn left soon after into White Rose Candles.

Although appearing to be of Georgian style, the bridge here probably dates back to the fifteenth century. There is a cascading waterfall immediately below, one that can be viewed from below by walking

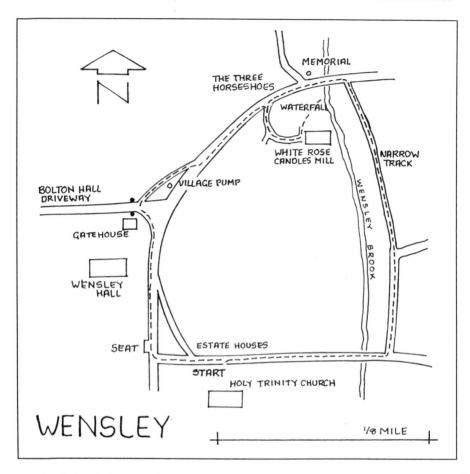

N

THE THREE
HORSESHOES

MEMORIAL

WATERFALL

WHITE ROSE
CANDLES MILL

NARROW
TRACK

BOLTON HALL
DRIVEWAY

VILLAGE PUMP

WENSLEY BROOK

GATEHOUSE

WENSLEY
HALL

SEAT

ESTATE HOUSES

START

HOLY TRINITY CHURCH

WENSLEY

⅛ MILE

to the left of the Candle Workshop and following a narrow track to the foot of the fall.

White Rose Candles are made on the premises by Jen and Mick White, together with daughter Rachael. They produce a gorgeous selection of plain and scented candles in a multitude of shapes and sizes.

The showroom is one half of the building, the manufactory the other. And what a Heath-Robinson set-up it is too. All built by Mick, it may look like string and old bicycle wheels but it does exactly what they want: produce objects of symmetry and beauty.

The family started making candles in Leeds back in 1971, moving to this old water mill in 1978. Admission is free and the place is open

10am to 5pm every day except Wednesday and Saturday. Full details on 01969 623544.

¤ Return to the main road and turn left. Walk down here and turn left to reach the church.

Across the road, by the first junction is the local war memorial topped by a Celtic cross. The pub a few yards along is The Three Horseshoes, well worth a visit.

To the right is the imposing gateway that is the entrance to Bolton Hall. It's well over a mile down the drive, but it is a public right of way should you feel disposed to extend the walk through beautiful fields and trees, with the Ure never very far away.

Further down the road is Wensley Hall. This is a private residence and surrounded by walls and a hedge. Set into the wall is a recess that holds a seat. This is provided "...in memory of Victoria Orde-Powlett who loved her friends in the Dales and pities all wayfarers. All Saints Day 1930 aged 33 years."

Close By

A visit to nearby Castle Bolton is a "must". The village is dominated by the castle. Note the reversal of names; Bolton Castle is in Castle Bolton.

Richard, the first Baron Scrope of Bolton was Chancellor of England when, in 1379, he started to build Bolton Castle. It would be twenty years in completion. The building's style was ruled by the transition then under way between pure castle, built with defence in mind, and grand baronial residence where security was secondary, reflecting the increased peace of the time.

The family were well connected and are mentioned by William Shakespeare in three of his plays: Richard II, Henry IV and Henry V. They appear in history books regularly between the fourteenth and seventeenth century: frequently on the "wrong" side.

Bolton Castle, best described as a fortified manor house, was a grand structure that has survived the depredations of the centuries – including a Civil War siege – very well. Still owned by the present Lord Bolton, over the centuries it has acquired a fund of tales. One, almost inevitably, concerns Mary Queen of Scots. On July 15th 1568, she was brought to the castle, ostensibly as a guest, but in reality, the prisoner of Elizabeth I.

That she lived in some style is beyond doubt. Contemporary reports tell of a large retinue of servants, and her personal ceremonial tapestry displayed on the wall of the Great Hall. She was there for six months before being moved, eventually to end her days on the scaffold at Fotheringhay Castle in 1587.

Another legend attached to this lady – who must have been imprisoned in pretty well every castle in England during her time – is retailed during Trail 21.

Inside, today, amongst other things you can see Mary's bed chamber, The Great Chamber, the Armourers Forge and a Horse Mill.

The place is open to visitors between March and November from 10am to 5pm. Admission is £3 for adults, £2 for children and senior citizens.

The village church of Bolton-cum-Redmire is St Oswald, opposite the castle and worth a good look round, whilst the village post office next door is quite the most quaintly-housed one in the Dales. This ancient building, heavy with stone roof tiles, has a climbing tree growing outside and a mail box marked VR, making it well over a century old.

Trail 24: Middleham

Various appellations applied to Middleham from early days to the present include The Loyal, Royal Ancient, Township, The Windsor of the North, The Newmarket of the North. The story of Middleham is inextricably linked with Royalty and racehorses. The castle which dominates the scene is visited during the Trail, racehorses *en passant*. But evidence is all around. This is the premier area in the north of England to look for racehorses in training; well over two hundred at the last count. You will be most unlucky to visit Middleham without seeing some of these expensive beasts being paraded, moved or exercised. This is wall-to-wall horse country, providing a degree of employment in the place, the last word used advisedly. Talk to the locals and they call Middleham "their town". But it hardly seems big enough to qualify for that appellation.

Middleham is also one of several places visited during the course of these Trails that is, by common consent, part of the Dales whilst still being without the National Park boundary; albeit by only a mile or so in this case. It could so easily have been included in the original scheme had that boundary stuck to the banks of the river Ure. Whatever, given the scenery hereabouts, there is nothing to distinguish it from the "real" Park.

Trail Facts

Distance:	½ mile
Clean Shoe Rating:	8
Map:	O.S. Landranger Series No 99
Start:	Market Square, Middleham
Starting Grid Ref:	SE 127878
Car Parking:	In the square
Refreshment:	All around the square
Nearest TIC	Thornborough Hall, Leyburn, North Yorkshire DL8 5AB – 01969 23069.

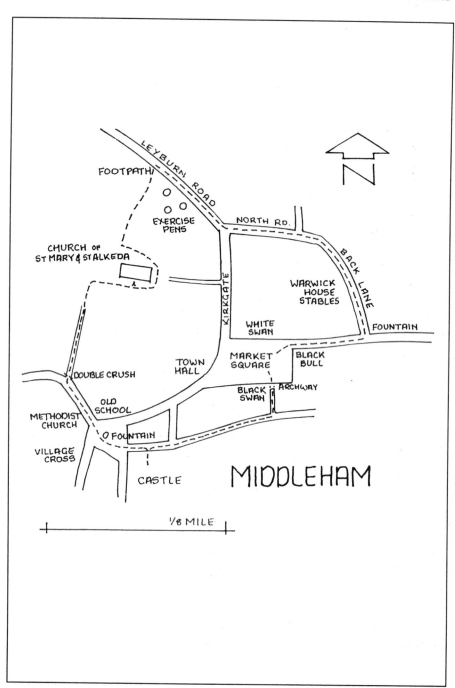

The one thing Middleham is not without is pubs. They surround the square and add a lovely character to it. The Black Swan is opposite The White Swan, and The Richard the Third.

¤ Walk down the Ripon road, past the Back Bull towards the edge of town and turn first left.

On the corner is an old cast iron drinking fountain whilst over the wall are some rudimentary horse jumps. The reason for these will become clear soon.

¤ Continue along Back Lane. This eventually turns left and becomes North Road. At the end of here, turn right.

There are stables on both sides of the road now. This is Warwick House Stables, owned by the noted trainer George Moore. Dozens of sleek equine heads peer curiously around half-doors and the perfume/reek/stench (depending on your preferences) of horses and manure pervade the area.

It is the wide open gentle slopes around the town that make it so popular for racehorse training. This is not new either. The monks of Jervaulx Abbey are credited (if that is the word) with establishing the tradition of breeding and training racehorses here. The author Charles Kingsley who was appointed honorary Canon in the church here in 1845 remarked on the number of jockeys and grooms in the town.

¤ Walk down Leyburn Road and some three hundred yards (270m) along, a Public Footpath sign points the way left.

On the left, more horse interest. This time, large circular pens constructed from old railway sleepers form exercise areas for the beasts.

¤ Walk along here into the church yard, turn left and circle the building to the door of the opposite wall.

The Church of St Mary and St Alkelda has served Middleham since the thirteenth century. There is some exquisite woodworking to be seen. At the rear of the church, a tall delicately carved cover sits over the font.

Nearer the altar are wooden stalls, again, ornately decorated by some wonderful old craftsman, stalls provided for the dean and canons.

These came from Richard of Gloucester when he arranged for collegiate status. More about the future Richard III later.

Over the centuries the chapter fell into disuse, revived only briefly during the nineteenth century before lapsing for ever in 1856.

Safely housed inside a glass case is a replica of The Middleham Jewel. This ancient reliquary was found near the castle, buried well beneath the surface, in 1985. It's a diamond-shaped pendant with a large sapphire inset, on a gold chain. An engraving of the nativity is shown on the reverse, one from the Trinity on the front.

As a relic, it's priceless. An intrinsic value of £2.5m was placed on it in 1991 when the Yorkshire Museum in York appealed for that amount to save it from being sold abroad. The sum was raised and the original now has a safe home there.

¤   Leave the church and turn right, following the path around to the left and into a narrow alleyway. At the top of here is a squeezer stile with dual passageways. Turn left beyond and walk to the main road and a square opposite the castle.

Across from the squeezer stile is Middleham Methodist Church whilst around the corner to the left is a delightful old school, complete with huge castellated tower. The building was erected..."in memory of Rev. James Birch, rector of Middleham by grateful parishioners and friends as an enduring monument of their esteem and affection and in fulfilment of his wishes, dedicated as a public school AD1869." This is now converted to The Old School Arts Workshop.

Close by is an ornate drinking fountain erected in 1887 to celebrate the Golden Jubilee of the reign of Queen Victoria. Across the road, more remains of great antiquity. The village cross, partially ruined, was believed to have been presented by Richard of Gloucester to mark the granting of market status to Middleham.

¤   Walk directly across the road towards the castle.

The present Middleham Castle is actually the second. The original was of motte and bailey construction and located to the south of the present ruin. It dates back to the initial years of the Norman conquest.

Its replacement was begun about 1170. The construction was huge – one of the largest in England. The inhabitants of this place have included Richard III who lived here as a young man under the tutelage of Earl of Warwick. Having married the Earl's daughter Anne, their son, Edward, was actually born here. The family lived in the castle until Richard was crowned in 1483.

This was a particularly turbulent and bloody time for England. The Wars of the Roses (a name not used until the nineteenth century when Sir Walter Scott coined it) had been simmering for years, occasionally breaking out into violence.

The house of York had the ascendancy for many years. Then, Edward IV died in 1483 leaving a child (Edward V) as heir. Then, a fatal split in the Yorkist clan saw Richard seize the throne. He was also believed to be responsible for the deaths of Edward and his brother Richard, famed as "the princes in the tower."

Whatever the truth, this created a massive rift throughout the country. The result was that, in 1485, Henry Tudor, the Lancastrian claimant fought with Richard at the Battle of Bosworth Field, slaying the Yorkist and ensuring that the house of Lancaster would ever be supreme. This, incidentally, was the last time the crown of England changed hands on a battlefield.

Middleham Castle never recovered from its association with Richard. It was allowed to fall into disrepair and was vandalised by the forces

The ruins of Middleham Castle

of the Lord Protector during the Civil War, ostensibly to prevent its further use.

Fortunately, there are still ample remains that give a vivid impression of the brooding glory that once was. It is today under the stewardship of English Heritage.

¤ Leave the castle and turn right. Follow this narrow road down, actually running alongside the square. On the left, passing Brind Cottage, an arrow points towards the toilets. Turn here, down a beautiful narrow alleyway with much ancient stonework to be seen, under the arch and back into the square and the starting point.

Trail 25: Richmond

Have I saved the best until last? An arguable comment which depends entirely on what you look for. Gone are the harsh dales, the stark scenery and the rushing watercourses. In their place, multifaceted history, elegant buildings, rolling grassy slopes all around and a real, live town.

Richmond is as close to the Dales National Park as it is possible to get without actually being in. The boundary finishes on the very edge of town, the furthest east it gets. If Skipton (Trail 2) guards the southern approach to the Dales, then Richmond most assuredly marks the north eastern flank. Again, the strategic importance of this location was recognised by early Norman visitors, searching for a defendable base from which to launch their subjugation of the locals. And a most commanding spot they selected, high on a cliff overlooking the river Swale.

It has remained prosperous over the centuries, a fact manifested in the abundance of fine housing to be seen at almost every turn. The place was visited over three centuries ago by that doughty female traveller Celia Fiennes. She found Richmond..."all stone, and the streets are like rocks."

Trail Facts

Distance:	1½ miles
Clean Shoe Rating:	10
Map:	O.S. Landranger Series No 92
Start:	Swimming Pool Car Park, Rimington Avenue, Richmond
Starting Grid Ref:	NZ 175009
Car Parking:	As above
Refreshment:	All around the town centre
Nearest TIC	Friary Gardens, Victoria Road, Richmond, North Yorkshire DL10 4AJ – 01748 850252

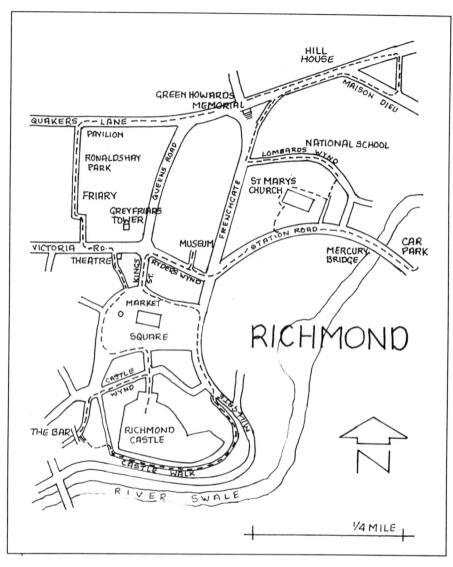

¤   Leave the car park, cross the attractive bridge over the Swale and
    head towards town. The road starts to climb and as it does so, the
    fine buildings of Richmond Lower School, formerly the Grammar
    School, can be seen on the left. As the road bears left, take the
    path off to the right that leads into St Mary's church.

This is a really grand building. Although showing examples of architecture spanning nine hundred years, most of the present form is by that famed Victorian architect Sir Gilbert Scott.

The choir stalls are particularly elegant, having been salvaged from nearby Easby Abbey after the Dissolution. These have misericords, again beautifully carved.

Much other woodwork in St Mary's comes from the works of Robert Thompson at Kilburn near Thirsk. Known as "The

The home of the regimental museum of the Green Howards

Mouse Man", each of his works has a trademark tiny mouse carved somewhere on it. The reredos is a fine example of the company's work.

The Green Howards Chapel is dedicated to that famous army regiment, based a few miles down the road at Catterick. Their presence will be noted a various points around this walk.

¤ Leave the church, turning right and circling around the rear of the building through the graveyard. At the bottom, where the path splits, take the left-hand one, past a stone which marks the re-founding of Richmond School in 1567, to the road. Turn left, up

Lombards Wynd. This is a steep climb past an elegant stone building on the right.

This was The National School erected in 1825, rebuilt and enlarged in 1894.

¤   At the top, turn right into Frenchgate and bear right along the cobbled surface to join the main road. On the left is a gateway giving entrance into Hill House.

An owner of this house, around two hundred years ago was William l'Anson and his family, one of whom was a daughter, Frances. She was actually born in Leyburn but soon moved here. Her name is probably quite unfamiliar; as it should be. She was never famous in her own right, but was immortalised by her husband Leonard McNalley whom she met after moving to London. He was moved to write:

> *This lass so neat,*
> *With smile so sweet,*
> *Has won my right goodwill.*
> *I'd crowns resign*
> *To call her mine.*
> *Sweet lass of Richmond Hill.*

This very house had further – albeit somewhat tenuous – connections with verse. In the nineteenth century, the house was rented by Sir Noel Milbanke. His daughter was the hapless bride of the poet Lord Byron, and had to compete with his half-sister for Byron's love.

¤   At the next junction bear right down Maison Dieu for a short distance. On the left is an ancient house dated 1797. Alongside this is an alleyway. Walk up here, admiring another wonderful old building before turning left, back down the hill.

On the left, actually at the top of Frenchgate is a war memorial dedicated to the memory of Green Howards regiment soldiers who died in battle.

Looking towards the left is a view over towards the church and the fine countryside beyond.

¤   Cross to the right-hand side whenever convenient and bear right along Quakers Lane as the main road disappears left. Along here, a wooden pavilion on the left marks the location of a narrow gateway in the wall. Turn here into Ronaldshay Park.

The old, boarded up, building, well concealed by hedges on the left is the friary.

¤   At the end of this path, exit to the road under an ancient stone archway and turn left, walking down to the narrow Friars Wynd on the right.

Note a delightful neo-Gothic pub on the right. The Fleece Hotel is all bowed windows and turrets. Some windows open on to Friars Wynd and it is possible to see that the inside is styled in a similar fashion.

A few yards further down the road are toilets and the Tourist Information Office.

On the corner of Friars Wynd is a gem of a building. The Georgian Theatre produced its first show in 1788 with the famous actor/manager Samuel Butler and continued in use until the 1840s. It then saw use for a variety of purposes, one of which was the storage of waste paper during the last war. A fire at that time did – by some miracle – little damage.

In 1963 it re-opened, restored to its original condition. There are guided tours available from Easter to the end of October, an excellent way of examining this treasure. Note the decorated panels around the balcony. Some of those scenes from Shakespeare are originals. Now the oldest Georgian theatre in the country, is an experience not to be missed. Try to take in a show. It's fascinating, even if the original seating is rather less than sumptuous.

Along Friars Wynd is one of the few remaining sections of city wall that was built in 1313. Note also what appears to be a tramroad in the pavement. This was laid when the theatre was used as a store as a means of moving goods to and from the Market Square more easily.

¤   At the top of here, turn right and stroll around the Market Place. Pass the various shops, restaurants and pubs. Continue walking round the perimeter until reaching the Market Hall. Turn right here into Richmond Castle.

Under the care of English Heritage, this castle was first constructed by Alan the Red in 1071. It was never used for its designed purpose and by the mid 1500s was largely in ruins. More building took place and it was returned to military use in the nineteenth century and General Robert Baden-Powell, founder of the Scout movement, was one of the commanding officers.

During the Great War, conscientious objectors were remanded here, as were others in the 1939-45 war, although by then much of the previous century's rebuilding had been demolished.

Its ground area is huge although there is not a lot left to see, but Scolland's Hall has much interest. This was build as a fortified but comfortable residence, one of the earliest remaining such, built in 1080.

There is one local legend concerning a passage said to run from the castle to Easby Abbey, a mile down the river Swale. Lost for centuries, a group of soldiers found the entrance at the end of the eighteenth century. It was a very narrow entry, too big for the men so a drummer boy was located and despatched. He was told to beat his drum as he went so that the soldiers above could plot his route.

All started well until the soldiers reached Easby Wood. There, the drumming ceased. Nothing was ever heard – or seen – of that boy again. Down in the wood, a carved stone marks the spot of his last known location. The opening times are 10am to 6pm daily from April to October, 10am to 4pm other months.

¤   Leave the castle and take a left-hand turn into a cobbled alleyway, Castle Wynd. At the end this opens into a larger area. Ahead are two roads. Take the right-hand one and after a few yards bear left down a narrow cobbled – again – lane. Down here is The Bar.

This is the last survivor of the original five postern gates that gave entry to the town.

¤   Here, as the road continues downhill under the Bar, bear left. This leads uphill to the foot of the castle wall. Swing round to the right along Castle Walk.

Across the valley is an ornate octagonal shaped Culloden Tower. It is a folly, built to mark the English victory over the Jacobites at Culloden Field in 1745.

Castle Walk was built in 1782 as a fashionable Georgian promenade for people to walk and take in the glorious views. It was previously known as The Terrace.

¤ Continue round the foot of the wall, admiring the view down below and noting that there is a sheer drop and no fencing. The river Swale gurgles on its way to the sea as the path eventually swings left again to join Millgate which returns the Trail to the bottom of the Square.

¤ Walk anti-clockwise around the perimeter to the corner of King Sreet. Here, cross the road – left – towards Holy Trinity Chapel.

In the bottom corner, outside Woolworth's is a delightful octagonal pillar box inscribed VR. Note The Castle Tavern which has served ale since 1806 and The Kings Head, an elegant three story pub.

Richmond's oldest church has a far greater history than that connected with religion. Over the years it has been used as an assize court, a prison, a school and even a granary. In 1973 it was converted to its present use, housing The Green Howards Museum.

A three-hundred-year story of this famous local regiment. You can see a unique collection of uniforms, war relics, archive film and a huge collection of medals including eighteen Victoria Crosses won by members of the Regiment for supreme gallantry.

That this area has always attracted the military is plain to see in the town. Look at the young men wandering around. Many are serving soldiers. Catterick, the name feared by successive conscripts during the days of National Service, is only a few miles away. Even today, it is still a very active army base.

¤ Return to King Street and walk to the bottom, turning right into Ryders Wynd.

Across to the left, in a park is Greyfriars Tower, the only remaining part of a Franciscan monastery that was established here in the mid 1200s. Why it remained after the Dissolution is not recorded, but it is known that it was only started in 1500 and was not complete by the time Henry VIII's edict was enforced.

¤ Walk down Ryders Wynd almost to the bottom where, on the left, The Richmondshire Museum is located.

Outside the museum, there is a large drinking fountain. This was originally located in the market place and stood on the site of a much earlier Georgian one. It was erected in 1904 to commemorate the sixty-three year reign of Queen Victoria.

It was removed from its location in 1958 and, fortunately, not destroyed. The opportunity to re-site it where it could be seen to best advantage was taken in 1987.

The Cruck House there contains medieval upper crucks removed from an ancient house in nearby Ravensworth in 1978. They were donated to the District Council and re-erected here in 1986.

Also on display is a set of James Herriot's surgery, as used in the TV series "All Creatures Great and Small". More on this subject can be discovered on Trail 17. Together with lots of other local interest, this is a place not to miss. It's open daily from 11am to 5pm from Good Friday to the end of October and a small admission charge is payable.

¤   Leave the museum, return to Ryder's Wynd and continue down to the bottom where the Trail turns left into Frenchgate. On reaching the main road, turn right and walk down the hill back towards the car park.

Easby Abbey, mentioned earlier, was another place that so impressed Turner that he committed it to canvas. The resulting water-colour captures the essential spirit of the place, showing that the walls which lean so precariously today were at a similar angle in his day.

Index

Swale, River   92
Swaledale Woollens   97

T

Tan Hill Inn   95
Tanner Hall   55
The Herriot Trail   89
The Pennine Way   44, 58, 92
The Ribble Way   58
The Waterfalls Walk   68
Theatre Cottage   29
Thompson, Robert   127
Threshfield   23
Turner, J.M.W.   8, 103, 113

U

Upper Wharfedale Museum   29

V

Vanbrugh, John   22

W

Wensley   114 - 115, 117
Wensley Hall   117
Wensleydale   76
Wensleydale Archers   91
Wensleydale cheese   79
West Burton   109, 111, 113
Wharfedale   24
Whernside   49, 71
White Abbey   20
White Rose Candles   115
White Scar Caves   70
Wight, Alf   88
Wordsworth, William   37

Y

Yore Mill Craft Shop   113

Z

Zion Congregational Church   55

More books on the Dales from Sigma Leisure:

YORKSHIRE DALES WALKS WITH CHILDREN

Local author and geography teacher, Stephen Rickerby, has devised over 20 walks to occupy children and their parents while walking in the Yorkshire Dales. Each walk has a check-list of things to look out for and there are useful notes for parents to discuss with children along the way. With the clear instructions in this book, and special entries to entertain young walkers, parents need never again hear the familar cry "Do we have to go for a walk?"
– with this book in their hands, children will actually want to go walking! £6.95

TEA SHOP WALKS IN THE YORKSHIRE DALES

Here are 30 gentle, circular walks from Yorkshire-born Clive Price to enjoy at a leisurely

pace. Take your time and enjoy the enormous diversity of landscape from impressive, high moorlands to lush green lanes and relaxing riverside paths.

There are routes to suit all ages and experience including family groups. Helpful notes on local and natural history add to the enjoyment. The walks are both an entertainment and an education: learn about local customs and colourful characters of the Dales, together with the fascinating history of long ago – the ancient castles at Middleham and Bolton, and the ruined medieval abbeys of Fountains and Jervaulx.

Detailed instructions, clear maps and the author's own photographs will inspire you to explore the Dales and enjoy its unique blend of teashops. £6.95

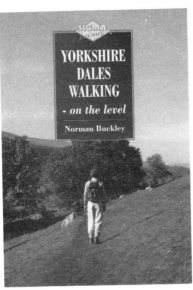

YORKSHIRE DALES WALKING - ON THE LEVEL

Another "on the level" book by writer and photographer Norman Buckley. This companion to Norman's Lake District guides has all the pleasures of the dales without the climbs "..a great buy" ILKLEY GAZETTE. £6.95

BEST PUB WALKS IN THE YORKSHIRE DALES

The title says it all – Clive Price knows just as much about Dales pubs as the tea shops! £6.95

All of our books are available from your local bookshop. In case of difficulty, or to obtain our complete catalogue, please contact:

Sigma Leisure, 1 South Oak Lane, Wilmslow, Cheshire SK9 6AR
Phone: 01625 – 531035; Fax: 01625 – 536800
E-mail: sigma.press@zetnet.co.uk;
Web site: www.sigmapress.co.uk
ACCESS and VISA orders welcome – use our 24 hour Answerphone service! Most orders are despatched on the day we receive your order – you could be enjoying our books in just a couple of days. Please add £2 p&p to all orders.